INDIAN SILVERWORK
OF THE SOUTHWEST
ILLUSTRATED

VOLUME ONE

by

HARRY P. MERA

DALE STUART KING, *Publisher*
Tucson, Arizona
1974

Printed in The United States of America
MONITOR PRINTING, INC. – TUCSON, ARIZONA

To the late Dr. Harry P. Mera (1875-1951), whose merry wit, rigid intellectual honesty, scholarly attainments, and shining personality enshrined him forever in the hearts of those who were fortunate enough to know him, this posthumous volume is affectionately dedicated.

Foreword

The object of this publication is to demonstrate through the medium of pictorial representations, the progress of evolution and various developments in Southwestern Indian silverwork from the early simple forms up to some of the later and more complex styles. There is presented in visual form sufficient material to make plain to those unfamiliar, or only slightly acquainted with the subject, the versatility and skill eventually achieved by the Indian craftsman.

The course taken by the craft is followed as closely as possible from its inception to no further than the late 1930's. This restriction was imposed because after that time the evils of commercialism may be seen to be adversely affecting the art. This, together with obvious trends toward radical changes in ideas on styles, has made the situation too difficult to define or evaluate at present. [As of 1940. Ed.]

Because reliance is placed so heavily on illustration, the text has been condensed to the essentials only. For those whose growing interest in the subject may demand more detailed and extended accounts, the works of a few other authors are available. Especially recommended is John Adair's THE NAVAJO AND PUEBLO SILVER-SMITHS, University of Oklahoma Press, 1944, which has an excellent biibliography, and Arthur Woodward's A BRIEF HISTORY OF NAVAJO SILVERSMITH-ING, Bulletin No. 14 of the Museum of Northern Arizona, Flagstaff, 1946.

Material used for illustrative purposes has been largely selected from the unusually comprehensive collections of the Indian Arts Fund and the Laboratory of Anthropology in Santa Fe, New Mexico. To these institutions and to Frank O. Packard, sr., also of Santa Fe, who kindly furnished a number of items, the writer wishes to express his sincere thanks.

H. P. M., 1940

ADDITIONAL NOTE

Eight years have passed since the foregoing was finally completed. At that time fashions in silverworking in the Southwest had fallen into a state of flux with no predictable trends, but in the interim, between then and now, the situation has become more stabilized. At the present a generalized pattern has emerged in which the treatment accorded silverwork is almost entirely based on the old Zuni predilection for a profusion of turquoise, with silver serving principally as a medium for mounting. Another disturbing factor is that traditional Navajo design appears no longer to occupy a position of importance. This, together with an increasing adoption of ideas, intrusive from sources outside the area, threaten eventually to destroy most of the Indian character of the art. Should such a condition continue to prevail, the native craftsman, in the end, may have to compete on no more than equal terms with his Caucasian counterpart.*

* See Editorial Postscript, p. 120.

H. P. M., 1948.

ACKNOWLEDGEMENTS

Acknowledged with pleasure is the generous permission of the Museum of New Mexico, Wayne R. Mauzy, director, to reprint Sections 1, 2, and 3 which first appeared as copyrighted Laboratory of Anthropology General Series Bulletins Nos. 17 and 18 (1944), and 20 (1945), respectively. The late author was then a staff member of the Laboratory.

The majority of photographs were taken by Stanley A. Stubbs, curator of the Laboratory of Anthropology, but after the Laboratory became inactive as an independent organization, the remaining illustrations were accomplished by Ruth Bernard of New York and Wyatt Davis of Santa Fe.

Circumstances prevented the publication of the good doctor's manuscript, despite its sterling worth, until this late date. However, since his painstaking work was historical in character, the value of his contribution to the knowledge of this intriguing subject is not lessened by its delayed appearance.

D. S. K.

Contents

Silver Mounted Bridles

After the Navajo and Zuni Indians of New Mexico and Arizona had learned, toward the end of the 1860's, to work silver, many articles of daily use, besides those intended for personal adornment, were handsomely embellished with that metal. Among the most striking in appearance were some of their horse trappings, particularly that part of a bridle known as the headstall.

The materials from which these bridles were made ranged from expertly braided buckskin to commercially tanned leathers, the silver ornaments being added in varying amounts and in different fashions. Suitably shaped objects in both wrought and cast silver were employed for such purposes. Although silver was by far preferred, brass and copper are known to have been occasionally utilized.

During the early days of silversmithing by these people, the methods of applying designs to metal were largely confined to a process of filing and to attempts at engraving, or sometimes, more properly, incising. On other occasions the abrading surface of a file was impressed on the metal to give a textured effect. Later, stamping by means of dies was introduced, which made possible a much greater degree of elaboration. Still later, repoussage, a kind of embossing, became popular.

The following plates feature examples selected from collections in the Laboratory of Anthropology. These will give some idea as to what part silver played, during past years, in the ornamentation of headstalls. These are shown spread flat. When in use a bit was suspended between the ends of the two longest straps.

PHOTOGRAPHS BY STANLEY A. STUBBS

1

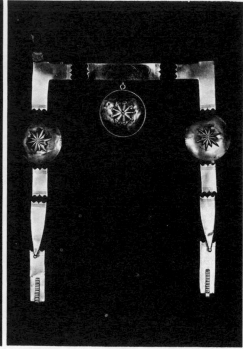

PLATE 1

This example illustrates one of the simplest, (if not the most simple) forms of the application of silver ornaments to headstalls. The metal is almost as thin as paper, indicative of a time when silver was a scarce article and a little had to go a long way. In consequence, it has been badly dented in places. When first obtained, the straps of which the bridle itself was composed were in such a state of disintegration that remounting was necessary. Though undated, narrow borders of scratched decoration near the ends of the various sections to be found only on early silverwork, appear satisfactorily to place its age.

PLATE 2

Another headstall is shown in which very thin gauge silver was used, including the two round conchas and a circular pendant. Outside of the stellate figures superimposed on the conchas and a medallion on the pendant, all decoration consists of narrow bands, close to the ends of the various sections, comprised of superficially scratched lines. It is believed that the two stellate forms and the medallion may have been added later, because the latter demonstrates some designs made by the use of dies, a technique coming into use following a fashion for incising. With these exceptions, evidence makes it appear probable that this bridle belongs to a comparatively early period of the craft.

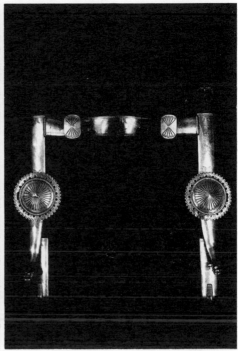

Well authenticated information attributes this specimen to the work of one Adsiti Chon, a noted Navajo silversmith who plied his t r a d e during the 1870's. Simplicity is the keynote here, only elemental, crudely engraved b o r d e r decoration providing relief to an otherwise marked severity of treatment. A loop at the lower border of the central concha on the brow-band indicates the former suspension of some sort of pendant. Note the tapering, silver-covered tabs extending downward from the cheek-straps which terminate in ornaments resembling the human hand.

Again a headstall of an earlier style has presumably received both new and additional decorative units subsequent to its making. While nothing but incised patterns are to be found on the original sections of silverwork, the two large conchas, as well as the round-cornered rectangular pieces on the brow-band, show designs produced by dies. It is on these differences in treatment that the above premise becomes possible. No provision was made, in this instance, for hanging a pendant from the brow-band. The two narrow straps, one ending in a small buckle, extending inward from the conchas, are parts of a throatlatch.

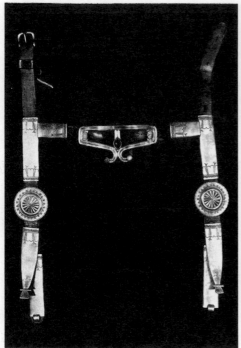
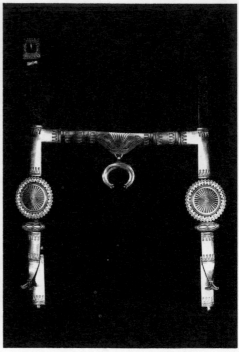

PLATE 5

The special feature of interest in this example is seen in the unusual openwork section occupying the center of the browband. This is composed of paired, wrought silver elements soldered at the back to a plate at either end. It has been set with five turquoise, of a rather inferior grade, mounted in plain bezels. No incised designs appear, most having been accomplished with dies. There are a few lines made with a cold chisel and some considerable shaping by filing on the rayed device in the centers of both conchas. There was plainlly no intent of attaching a pendant.

PLATE 6

As time progressed a new and different decorative technique came into use on silverwork in the Southwest. This was a method, called repoussage, by which figures were produced in relief by hammering from the back. A portion of the central design occurring on the browband of the above example was made by such a process. All die work is of a very superior quality, being evenly spaced and impressed to a uniform depth throughout. The crescentic pendant is of a form greatly esteemed, not only for bridles, but one even more popular for use with necklaces. To the Navajo this is known as a *najahe*. The buckle at the top of the bridle is also of wrought silver.

4

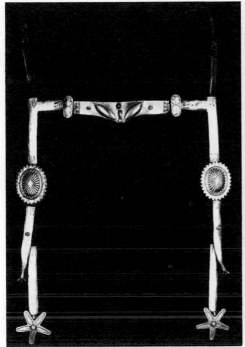

PLATE 7

PLATE 8

A marked delicacy distinguishes this headstall from any other as yet recorded. As noted for the preceding plate, figures in repousse occupy the central section of the browband, though in much higher relief. In addition three turquoise have been mounted on this same piece. Two other settings of that stone will be observed on the tabs depending from the cheekstraps, just beneath the conchas. Also deserving mention are the oval conchas, instead of the customary circular type. As a measure of further elaboration, two star-shaped button-like objects have been tied by thongs to the rings for attaching a bit. With the exception of the embossing, all other decoration is in die stamping. No pendant was apparently planned for.

In this instance practically every piece of the silver mounting, instead of being flat as shown by all the headstalls previously illustrated, has been longitudinally ridged in the center so as to be V-shaped in cross-section. Die work furnishes most of the ornamental effects, the only exceptions being motifs done in repousse on the browband and some highly embossed centers for the conchas. A pendant of some sort has evidently been removed or lost at some time in the past, because a loop showing wear was provided for hanging one of these objects.

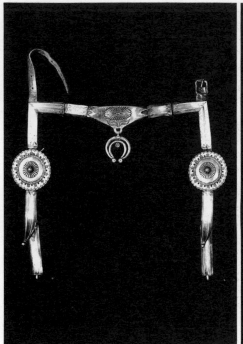

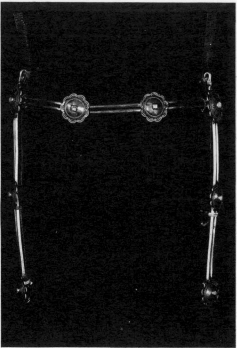

PLATE 9

The remarks accompanying the plate just preceding, with a little alteration, will apply equally to the example shown here. Only two important differences exist: instead of a single angular treatment for the silver mountings, a paralleling doubled arrangement has been substituted; and also that in this case a *najahe* pendant, set with a single turquoise, remains in place.

PLATE 10

The structural details of this headstall are quite unlike those of any other, so far coming to attention. Half-round s i l v e r bars, in pairs, compose the several sections which, instead of being applied in the usual manner directly on the l e a t h e r straps, are ingeniously hinged to one another, thus making the entire metallic structure an independent unit. This has been tied by buckskin thongs to an ordinary l e a t h e r headstall. Wherever the sections are joined by hinges, as well as at the two free ends, conchas set with turquoise have been soldered on so as to completely conceal those parts. Die work alone has been used for incidental designs.

6

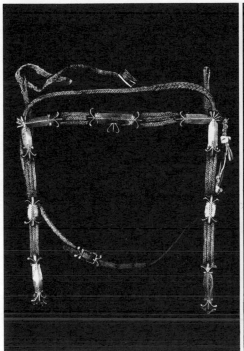

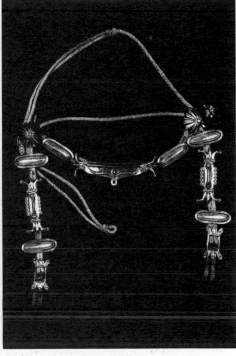

PLATE 11

PLATE 12

A lack of harness leather did not seem to present any particular problem, as buckskin for braiding a bridle was nearly always at hand. One of the braided sort appears above. Because of the flexibility and narrowness of such material, it was patently impossible to employ anything but silver ornaments of the smaller sizes. All decorative units seen here have been cast from that metal, including the two small buckles. A scattering of lunate impressions made with a die constitute the only attempts at a surface design. There is no provision for a pendant. Judging from the badly worn condition and friability of the braid, a respectable age can be safely postulated.

An example of a braided buckskin headstall which is notable for the number and elaborateness of its ornaments. There is included a considerable variety of silver o b j e c t s, both wrought and cast. On these much work with dies is in evidence. Three of these units are unusually ornate, one on the browband and one each on either cheekstrap. The first mentioned displays a loop for the suspension of a pendant. Turquoise settings may be seen on a number of the pieces. There can be little question but that this bridle is representative of a much later style than that shown on the preceding plate.

Bracelets: Filed and Stamped

The simplest form of silver bracelet made by the native smiths of the Southwest, following their adoption of the craft, was, as far as present evidence goes, merely a flat band of that metal decorated by means of filing or, more rarely, by incising. A little later, designs produced by stamping with homemade steel dies came into vogue. At a yet later date other techniques were employed to give rise to yet other styles. A discussion of these last, however, will be reserved for illustration and remarks at another time.

Although the first three methods cited above were the earliest practiced, it should not be thought that they were confined solely to the initial period of silverwork, as all have persisted to some extent and in some form to the present time.

Little exact data are available concerning the date when an additional embellishment was first attempted through the use of applied mounts holding settings of glass, abalone shell, unpolished garnets, turquoise and other oddments. A few references exist, as early as circa 1880, concerning the use of turquoise for such purposes. But from the scarcity of this type of adornment to be found on bracelets of manifestly early style, it appears unlikely that sets of any kind became particularly popular until around the beginning of the 20th century.

The examples here illustrated have been chosen to show a chronological development, extending from the most elemental forms to those of greater complexity, as well as late survivals of some of the older decorative techniques.

PHOTOGRAPHS BY STANLEY A. STUBBS

PLATE 1

At top and bottom of the plate are examples of narrow bracelet forms, perhaps more properly called bangles, upon which only files were used.

The central figure illustrates an early attempt at stamped work. A die making a small circular mark, similar to that which might be made with a leather punch, and another having a curved impression were all that were employed in the principal design.

Of this group, the two uppermost were secured from the effects of a trader, many years deceased. According to information furnished by his heirs, the two should date early in the 1880's or perhaps slightly earlier.

PLATE 2

The top band demonstrates the use of a very simple form of die, undoubtedly of home manufacture. The marginal ridges were made to stand out by filing away some of the metal toward the center of the bracelet. It was purchased in 1901 and was even then in a decidedly worn condition. There is a strong possibility that it may date almost as early as the stamped example on Plate 1.

The next in order below is plainly a not too successful attempt to get away from a standard style. There is no history but from the amount of wear and the fact that it was set with abalone shell instead of turquoise a fairly early dating may be postulated.

In the third specimen, although the die work is comparatively simple, the type of workmanship would definitely take it out of the earliest class and should place it somewhere next in line of development, probably in the 1890's.

9

PLATE 3

Here are t h r e e bracelets which prove that decorations produced by a method of filing, one of the earliest technigues used in Indian silver craft, have in no way become obsolete. The one in the center shows considerable ingenuity in the use of such a tool for getting an unusual and novel effect.

Upon examination of the topmost, it will be noted that the settings of turquoise had been put in place after the diagonal ridges had been filed. All of this group are comparatively late make.

PLATE 4

Occupying a central position on this plate is seen a very distinguished piece of rather recent die work. It has been so placed that direct comparisons may be made with the two accompanying bangles, in order to show differences with earlier stamped designs.

The band above it was originally secured in Las Vegas, New Mexico, about the year 1885. Three different noncommercial dies have been used in impressing the pattern. The leaf-shaped die is of particular interest, inasmuch as it was obviously fashioned from a section of the file.

The bangle at the bottom exhibits a somewhat later type of die work than that on the upper. It is mainly of interest because it shows that mounting with turquoise c a m e as an after thought, at least one of the little squares forming the design having had to be tooled down to make room for seating a bezel.

10

PLATE 5

No remarks on any particular detail are necessary for this plate, except to state that bracelets of this general style were the fashion for quite a number of years prior to the opening of the 20th century. Only a collection of dies and a cold chisel were required to produce every decorative feature to be seen here.

PLATE 6

An exuberance in stamped decoration does not appear to be confined to any one period of Southwestern Indian silverwork, but rather must be laid to the whim of some individual smith.

The upper of the two band bracelets shown here was secured from a family in whose possession it had remained since the later 1880's, whereas the lower was purchased in brand new condition in 1933. Possibly both may be a little ornate for some tastes, but this condition is perhaps overbalanced by the meticulously skillful workmanship displayed.

11

PLATE 7

The wide bracelet at the top is another example of the type in vogue during the same period as those illustrated on Plate 5 but is superior to them in craftsmanship, the die work being more precisely executed.

Below there appears a piece that, should the given date of about 1890, ascribed to it by the family of its former owner, be accepted, would be one of the earlier bracelets which had been planned for settings of turquoise. The character of the tooling strongly tends to verify such dating although mountings of this stone at that particular time are known to have been few and far between.

PLATE 8

The first quarter of the 20th century would, without question, cover the time interval during which all of the above bracelets were made. This selection was chosen to show variety in style as well as to call attention to the continuity of the techniques first employed in the early days of the art. The deep grooves seen in the uppermost specimen, on either side of the square turquoise set, were made with some sort of round file.

It was at this same period that commercialism began progressively, more and more, to influence the course of Indian silverwork. The resulting stimulation becomes evident in the large number of new shapes and the increased use of turquoise settings, both in number and size

PLATE 9

The members of this group also display characteristics that mark them as products of the same period as those represented on the preceding plate. For shaping the one at the top, it was necessary to file down much of the metal around the central portion in order to bring the rounded margins into relief. Next all of the die work was done, and finally a bezel for the turquoise mounting was affixed.

As for the bracelet in the center, the maker manifestly strove for a showy effect with a minimum of effort, the oval shaped piece being made separately and later soldered in place.

Note the tapering designs on the remaining example. Such a pattern must have required a set of dies graduated as to size.

PLATE 10

An unusually massive piece which shows to what extent, on occasion, ostentation in personal adornment could be carried. It weighs exactly one-half pound avoirdupois. Files, dies and a cold chisel were used in furnishing the decorative features. The turquoise chosen for the mountings is of a rather poor quality.

PLATE 11

This plate shows still another variant in band bracelet treatment. The example at the top illustrates the general idea most clearly. In this type the central section of a flat band, before being curved, is split into the desired number of divisions by means of a cold chisel. These are then spread apart and shaped with small files and some abrasive such as emery cloth. The method was used when an article of a lighter appearance was wanted. The two lower bracelets have later had stamped ornamental devices and turquoise mounts applied over the divisions. In the lowermost mount a drilled stone was utilized, one which very evidently had previously been worn as an earbob.

PLATE 12

The bracelets shown on this plate possess one thing in common. They are composite, being made up of separate units variously held in place to form a whole. There is considerable disparity in regard to age between the three. The upper one, composed of three members, bears a date of 1887. Die work alone was used for ornamentation. Three vertically placed strips of silver have been attached with solder to hold the several parts immovable. One strip was placed in the center on the inner surface and two externally at either end.

The center one also shows a triple arrangement. In addition to narrow vertical end-sections the turquoise mountings by means of solder hold everything together. Doubting the ability of his bezels to hold the sets firmly, the artificer drilled each stone so that a silver peg inserted and fastened to the bracelet secures them in position. It was probably made during the 1930's.

The lower, a two-member piece, shows signs of soldering along the line of juncture and in addition the decorated plate holding a turquoise acts as a further reinforcement. Evidence suggests manufacture early in the 20th century.

14

Bracelets with Embossed Designs

There are no specific data as to just when embossing and its more inclusive counterpart, repoussage, were first employed in the decoration of Southwestern Indian bracelets. Neither is it known where the craftsmen of that area acquired the technique. Three principal possibilities appear to exist.

One of these could have been a direct derivation from some Spanish or Mexican metal work, although as yet nothing has come to light to substantiate such a view.

Another source might stem from the custom of forcing small silver coins or disks into iron molds with a variety of dies to make hollow, dome shaped buttons, a kind much esteemed in the past by many Mexicans, who used them in large numbers for the adornment of their clothing. This same procedure is still utilized by the Indian smith when like objects are to be made.

The third possibility may spring from the occasionally-used expedient of giving a convex surface to a bracelet by pounding it into shape from the rear, a process probably primarily designed to give a very thin silver article an external appearance of greater weight.

Whatever the origin, repousse work, once adopted, became very popular during the 19th and up until the first quarter of the 20th centuries. It appears likely that repoussage came into use not long after die work became well established and when employed is normally combined with the latter technique.

PHOTOGRAPHS BY STANLEY A. STUBBS

PLATE 1

At the top is an example wrought from very thin silver, one which well illustrates the third of three possible origins for repoussage in the Southwest, as noted on the preceding page. The thinness of the metal suggests a relatively early date, such a view being further strengthened by information furnished by the former owners.

The next below it is of interest because of the scant amount of die work incorporated in the design. All embossed elements have been outlined by an impressed line.

The remaining specimen has an elongate lozenge-shaped figure at the front, in much lower relief than the average .

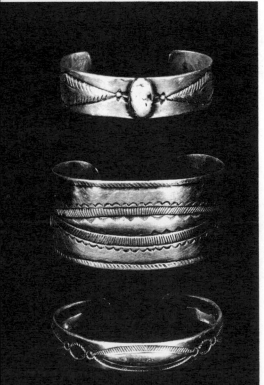

PLATE 2

The two upper bracelets illustrate additional examples of ornamentation in comparatively low relief. Of these, the uppermost is in a badly worn condition.

Inner surfaces at both ends of the one at the bottom show hollows produced by the hammering necessary to bring the several oval design elements into prominence. The obverse faces of the two toward the rear are only partially visible. This piece appears also to represent a fairly early stage in the development of native repousse work.

PLATE 3

Centrally placed bosses and other features in both repousse and stamped work were used in decorating all the bracelets figured here. The reverse aspects of two of the bosses may be seen close to the ends of the lowermost.

During the late 1920's, large numbers of this type were bought up by certain dealers in antique Indian silver, and, with a little shaping, were widely sold for use as napkin rings.

PLATE 4

A point of interest in this group is to be seen on the inner surface and near the extremities of the one at the bottom. In this instance, the smith, while embossing, evidently stretched the metal to such a thinness that the tops of the protuberances evidently became worn through, leaving irregular openings. The rear of two small bosses are also visible on the topmost, which has been further embellished by mountings of turquoise.

17

PLATE 5

Here are two demonstrations of outstanding craftsmanship in Indian silverwork; every feature displays good taste and skillful treatment.

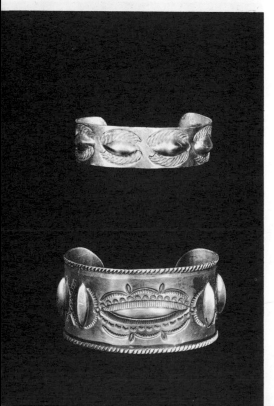

PLATE 6

Both of these bracelets, by reason of the quality of work, deserve a degree of praise e-qual to that given the two on the preceding page. Note espec-ially in the lower, the keeled bosses on either side of the cen-tral design of repousse and die work. Embossment of such ex-treme character was not often attempted.

18

PLATE 7

The principal interest in this illustration centers about the embossed stars on the upper specimen. To obtain such an effect with the few tools available to the average Indian silver worker was no mean accomplishment. Some stamping has been added to bring the stars into still greater prominence.

Below is an unusual form, though the decorative motifs are of the usual type.

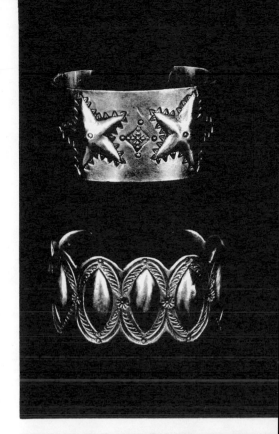

PLATE 8

At the top is an eccentrically designed piece. However, the q u a l i t y of repoussage and stamping demonstrates a pronounced nicety of execution.

Beneath this is one which is not only oddly shaped but is also unusually crowded with die impressions. Two pairs of narrow elongate bosses occur on either side of the central section, while dents near the ends mark the site of others. Eight small turquoise sets of several shapes are an additional decorative feature.

19

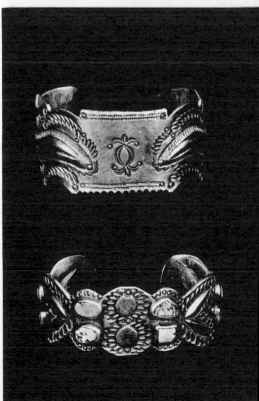

PLATE 9

The pair figured here is typical of this class, the lower having two highly elevated bosses, the other only repousse work. On the latter will be seen an elongate piece of turquoise, drilled at one end for suspension, which has been re-used as a set. A silver peg passing through the drilled hole and soldered to the bracelet helps, with the aid of a bezel, to hold the stone in place.

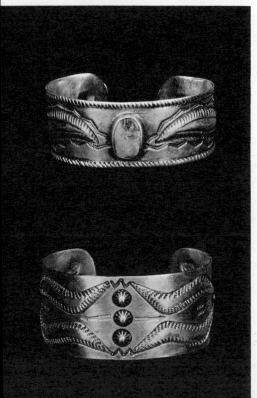

PLATE 10

Other examples of repoussage. Attention is called to the three small bosses appearing in the center of the lowermost. These are much like some of the buttons seen decorating Navajo costumes, though very much smaller in size. On either side of the bosses, arrows have been stamped. Dies of this sort were introduced by certain traders in the mistaken belief that articles on which they were used would look more "Indian".

20

PLATE 11

Heavy gauge silver is much more difficult to handle than that of medium thickness when designs in repousse were used. The bracelets shown here and others appearing on the following plate were wrought from unusually heavy metal. Considering the thickness, the maker has achieved a most creditable result, especially in the lower one, by far the heavier of the two, which weighs 5 ounces, avoirdupois. This system of weights is used instead of troy, because, for the average individual, it makes for a better comparison with articles of daily use, the weights of which often are known.

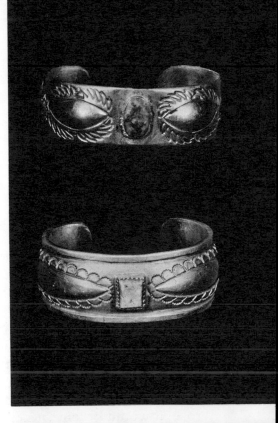

PLATE 12

In these two bracelets, it is plainly apparent that the silversmith was less successful in making a well-finished product. This is particularly evident in the lower example. From the top downward they weigh 4 and 4½ ounces (avdp.), respectively. Again are to be seen native cut turquoise, once worn as eardrops, converted into sets and reinforced by pins passed through holes drilled near their ends.

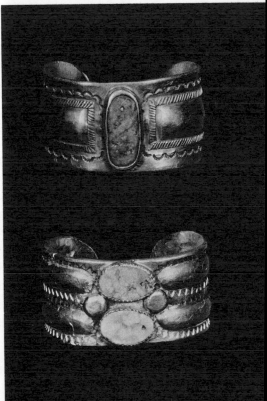

21

Cast Bracelets

The ratio of cast silver bracelets, in relation to the number of those wrought from that metal, has always been very low; this in spite of the fact that at least a rudimentary form of casting must have been practiced since the beginning of Indian silverworking in the Southwest.

Recourse to that process must have been required when an article was desired which demanded more material than that afforded by a single coin, coinage being the only source available to the early smith. When such a contingency a-rose, it would become necessary to melt a number of these together, the aggregate being poured into some sort of mold in order to yield a single workable ingot.

Most any sort of stone of suitable size and shape which was resistant to heat, and yet soft enough to be hollowed out to meet requirements, was undoubtedly used by the early artisan.

Later on, when, through experience, easily worked, fine-grained stones were selected (those capable of retaining clean cut impressions) ornamental casting finally came into its own. Materials of this sort, because of their friability, are apt to break down under the heat to which they are subjected so that, at best, a very limited number of castings could be made from the average mold, often only one. After an object is cast, a great deal of work with files and other abrasives is required to obtain a satisfactory finish.

Although few molded bracelets can be dated as early as the 1870's, the bulk of this order is comparatively late in the craft, with some being still produced at the present time.

PHOTOGRAPHS BY STANLEY A. STUBBS

22

PLATE 1

Two very early cast bracelets are shown here. Both on information obtained are ascribable to a time not later than the late 1870's. Molds for such as these entailed little effort at artistry. A broad groove was cut for the central band, from which side channels were made for casting the series of knobbed appendages occurring on either side. The upper specimen has been set with native garnets in the rough. Note the numerous tiny surface pits in the lower, a result of inexpert casting and finishing. All bracelets in the molded category are cast flat, being later reheated for the annealing necessary to curve them to fit the wrist.

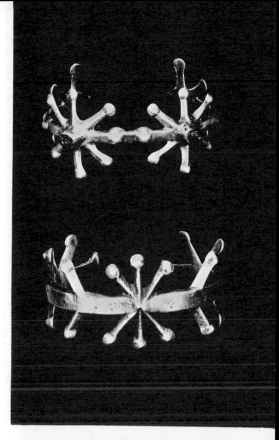

PLATE 2

Demonstrating a somewhat greater degree of refinement in ornamental casting, this pair is representative of a period but little later than those figured on the preceding plate. In the upper of the two the same basic form is again to be seen - a central bar with curved elements - while the other shows a somewhat greater degree of inventiveness. Some pitting of the surface is again apparent.

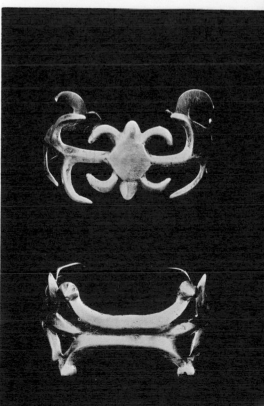

23

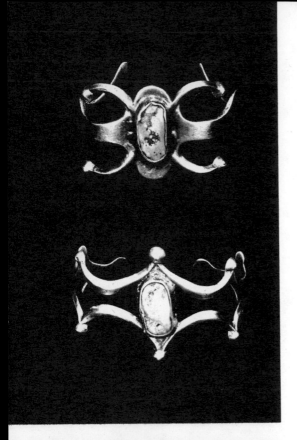

PLATE 3

Still derivatives of a comparatively early phase of casting, both of these examples have been set with turquoise, a rare happening at this stage of development. A certain lack of skill, probably due to unfamiliarity with the required procedure, is plainly apparent in the preparation and seating of the bezels for holding the hand-cut sets.

PLATE 4

By way of contrast, unset bracelets of up-to-date manufacture appear on this plate. The workmanship displays a familiarity with the v a r i o u s technical details involved.

There is fine tooling or milling along the edges of the carinated portions, at top and bottom of the upper one.

PLATE 5

At the top is a fairly recent example of unusually thin casting. The maker chose to mold it in two sections, apparently because of its delicacy. The joint where the two were soldered together has been concealed and strengthened by a mounting of turquoise. A length of twisted square wire has been carried around the center as an additional embellishment.

The bottom bracelet was cast at a single pouring.

PLATE 6

All of the lozenge-shaped devices and the three turquoise mounts (of which two are not visible) occurring on the upper specimen, have been soldered in place.

In the lower of the two illustrated here, another two-sectional casting treatment is once more exemplified. Also the joint is again covered and reinforced by a plate bearing a rectangular setting of some kind of dark green stone. This piece gives evidence indicating quite a respectable age.

PLATE 7

At the top of this plate is an ambitious but not too successful attempt to achieve an effect of marginal twisting, accomplished while carving the mold. This resulted in several weak spots in the cast article. Over these thin places, patches of silver have been neatly applied on the inner surface. A square-cut turquoise is mounted in the center.

On the one below it is shown, around the pear-shaped set, how stamping with dies was added for supplemental decoration. The crack seen below and to the left of the central area was due to incomplete annealing before shaping into bracelet form.

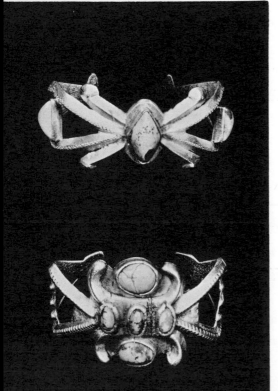

PLATE 8

A close inspection of the lower of the two bracelets shown here reveals another instance of cracking due to improper annealing. The break can be seen to the right of the central setting of turquoise. To remedy this defect, a fairly heavy silver plate, not only large enough to cover the crack but extending well outward on all sides, is used for a backing. The two largest sets at top and bottom are mounted on this plate.

Both examples show some simple tooling.

26

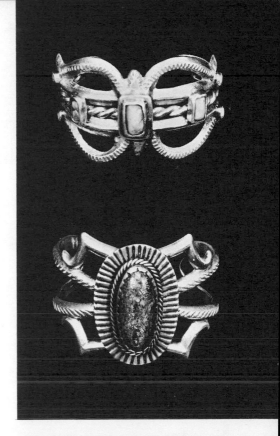

PLATE 9

The bracelet at the top of this illustration was planned so that a median, lengthwise slot was left open for the reception of a pair of wires twisted together - a combination yielding very pleasing results. Native-cut turquoise sets and a little tooling are accessory decorative details.

A wrought, tooled medallion has been affixed to the one at the bottom, on which is mounted an oval setting of some greenish stone, probably malachite. Series of die impressions have also been employed.

PLATE 10

The upper bracelet is one which was obviously designed especially to display a maximum amount of turquoise. There are 12 small sets and three of large size distributed at various points on its surface.

Below is a more conservatively designed piece. Encircling a central mounting of that same stone, four droplets of silver have been affixed at intervals.

27

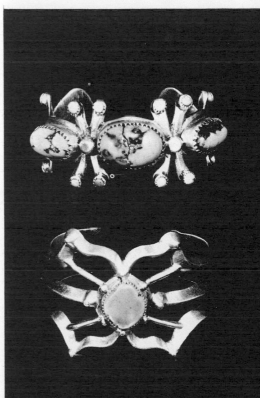

PLATE 11

This plate illustrates still other ideas in decorative casting, provision for all features of which, except for the turquoise mounts and die work, having had to be made when the molds were carved.

The bracelet in the center appears to have developed a weak spot while being curved. This has been reinforced at the back with a flattened piece of silver.

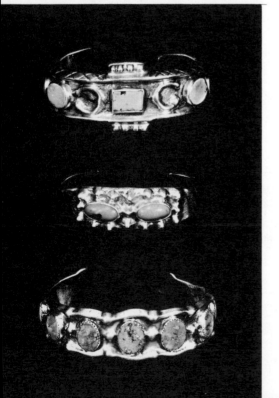

PLATE 12

The three specimens appearing here may be considered as constituting something in the nature of a subtype. Unlike the majority of cast bracelets, the principal thought seems to have been to produce figures of various sorts in bas-relief, instead of a more usual concern with open-work effects. Spaces between the several raised figures were reserved for the seating of bezels to hold turquoise sets.

28

Carinated Bracelets

Originating fully as early as that class of bracelets in which decoration was confined solely to file-work and incising is another bracelet category that deserves credit as being one of the basic types in the utilization of non-ferrous metals by the Indians of the Southwest. The form can be identified by its generally triangular cross-section, the apex pointing away from the wearer's wrist, thus producing a keeled or carinated effect. It is from this peculiarity that the term carinated bracelet has been coined for the group as a whole.

The style was probably suggested as a result of the casting of an ingot in a V-shaped groove as a preliminary to further shaping, perhaps to be hammered into a heavy rounded bangle or flattened into a band. It might be mentioned in passing that a channel of this shape would require the least effort to cut in the stones habitually used by the early smith for molding his silver. Thus the making of castings of this particular form could well have been a routine procedure when a narrow bracelet of most any sort was intended. Although in the beginning carinated bracelets appear to have always been cast, later, when the fashion received a full measure of popular approval, there is evidence to show that some were shaped by other methods.

In the oldest and simplest forms, the sole decoration consisted of series of diagonally placed parallel lines made with either a cold chisel or a file. Superseding this method, designs were produced almost exclusively by die-work. Still later, when bracelets of greater complexity began to be desired, matched pairs were frequently employed as foundations for many kinds of elaborations. Another derivative is to be seen in a very wide type of bracelet which simulates, in a single piece, the several separate bangles formerly worn simultaneously.

PHOTOGRAPHS BY STANLEY A. STUBBS

PLATE 1

At the top is shown one of the earliest and simplest forms of this style. The oblique markings were made with a cold chisel.

Next below it is another example, which differs only in bearing stamped designs.

For the lowermost, conical knobs at both extremities and a centrally located plate, extending out from both sides of the bangle, were provided for in the mold for casting. The latter feature is concealed by two plain bezels holding turquoise sets.

PLATE 2

Here are illustrated three methods of combining carinated units. Above, three undecorated members have been employed, the two outer being slightly tapered toward their ends.

In the center a pair of these units are joined by a length of twisted wire by soldering all together along their margins.

At the bottom, still another treatment has been used. The ends of two stamped elements were fastened at such an angle that a central space was opened for the insertion of an oval setting

PLATE 3

All bracelets on this plate are comprised of matched pairs. Note the notching of both carinas on either side of the central ornamental device on the upper specimen. In this case the two members are held slightly apart by vertical end-plates.

The two remaining examples, although their several p a r t s were fashioned separately, have been tightly joined in pairs by means of silver solder. A cross-like object mounted with turquoise and a great deal of tooling distinguishes the lower of these.

PLATE 4

For the topmost, two carinated elements flank a plain flat band. The whole is held firmly together by n a r r o w vertical strips soldered to the extremities and by four ornamental clamps. These latter were made to pass entirely around and firmly bind together all parts, thus eliminating any necessity for marginal soldering. The clamps are embellished with silver globules and turquoise.

Below are a pair of the two-unit type. The upper of these is reinforced at the ends with strips applied externally, while in the lower the same feature occurs on the inner surface. Further rigidity is obtained by inserting a row of rectangular turquoise sets.

31

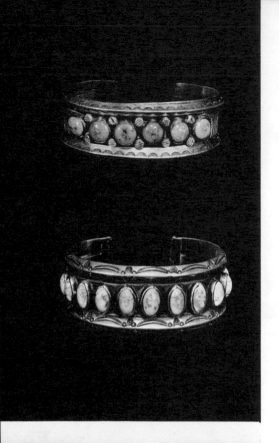

PLATE 5

The two figured on this plate are alike in having the intervals between the carinated parts filled in with bands of thin gauge silver, upon which rows of turquoise mountings have been applied.

A quite unusual treatment, that of stamping the globules which occur in alternation with the sets, may be seen on the upper of the two shown here.

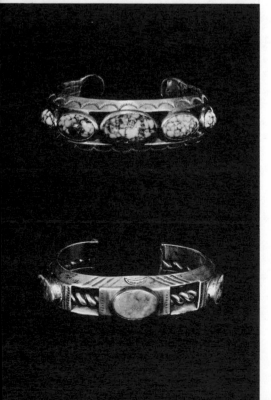

PLATE 6

Probably the most highly favored way of filling in the space between pairs of carinated units was by means of twisted wires of various sizes and sorts. Such an arrangement is clearly visible in the bracelet at the bottom but a like feature is almost completely concealed by the closely spaced s e t t i n g s which encircle the upper specimen.

PLATE 7

Other examples of the same general type as those shown on the preceding plate are pictured here. In addition to the silver wire centers, small balls and stamped bars of that metal have been interspersed here and there as added features.

PLATE 8

Although further demonstrating the use of twisted wire fillers, these bracelets differ in having double strands instead of the more usual single arrangement. This is plainly apparent in the lower of the two but cannot be seen in the picture of the one above it because of the superposition of an elaborate decorative device, bearing a circular turquoise set. This latter ornament has the appearance of being bordered by small twisted wires but this is merely an effect produced by tooling.

PLATE 9

For this pair, in order to take advantage of the space left open between the carinated elements for decorative purposes, wire has been discarded in favor of separate units of design and mounts of turquoise. Strips at the ends hold the principal structural parts in place and control the width of the opening.

PLATE 10

Triple arrangements of their carinated members characterize these examples. In the upper one all p a r t s including two lengths of twisted square wire were soldered tightly together. Notching of the carina belonging to the central member gives an appearance somewhat like that of the adjacent twisted wire.

The lower, on the contrary, has all the basic elements separated by narrow open spaces. Heavy terminal strips and an ornamental device bearing a turquoise set, once an earbob, provided rigidity.

34

PLATE 11

Aside from the applique ornaments - one having a sunburst effect, the other somewhat
cruciform in shape - both of
these specimen were cast in a
single piece. Bracelets of this
kind seem to have been originated to give an appearance similar to that of the several separate carinated bangles customarily worn in earlier times, but
without some of the disadvan-
tages of that fashion. The larger of the two weighs 8 ounces,
avoirdupois.

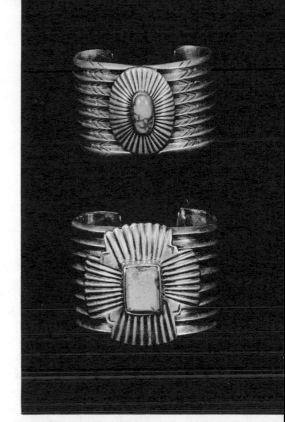

PLATE 12

Instead of being cast in one
piece like those shown on the
previous plate, the lower of the
two here pictured was made up
of separate circlets which were
then soldered to one another a-
long their margins. All but the
outer sections s h o w some
stamped decoration.

The upper example with the
applied "butterfly" design was
cast, aside from that feature, in
a single mold.

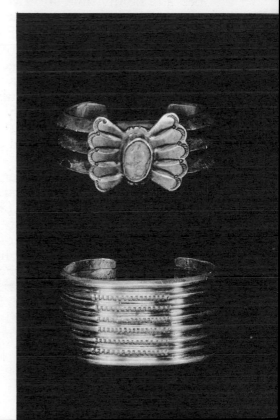

Bracelets of Wire

There exists a rather arbitrary definition of what properly constitutes a wire: one which limits the size to a diameter of not over three-sixteenths of an inch, anything above the figure being considered a rod. To most, the term refers to the more ordinary sort which has a circular cross-section, whereas in reality wire may have a number of shapes including those which are rectangular in section. The following remarks deal with bracelets employing material coming within the above specifications.

The use of wire by Southwestern Indian silversmiths appears to be divisible into two phases, an early one and another at a considerably later date. As yet nothing definite has turned up to indicate a transitional stage connecting the two. Although silver was at all times preferred, copper and brass were frequently utilized during both phases.

Many of the earliest bracelets were merely circlets of hand-shaped wire, occasionally slightly tapered toward the ends. Others, as often, only had the extremities rounded off. This early type was customarily decorated by a series of filed grooves or impressed grooves arranged to form simple patterns.

It was not until much later, long after these early bangles had practically disappeared, that wire bracelets again came into favor. So late in fact that nearly all of the type will be seen to have elaborate mountings of both silver and turquoise, a sure indication of a period not too long before the opening of the 20th century. At this time the large sizes of wire were still being forged by hand, though the smaller kinds clearly had been passed through a drawplate, which by then had been introduced. Still later commercially drawn wires have been incorporated in articles made by Indian labor in attempts at mass production.

PHOTOGRAPHS BY STANLEY A. STUBBS

PLATE 1

At the top is a very simple form of twisted wire bangle, for which, despite its simplicity, an early dating must not be taken for granted. It is, in fact, a non-commercial item of the late 19th century.

Both the next below and the one at the bottom are representative of the earliest known type. In both cases decoration was accomplished by means of a cold chisel or by filing. The latter of the two is made of brass.

The remaining example illustrates contemporary trends. All the wire used in this instance was factory made and merely issued to Indian workers for twisting and finishing.

PLATE 2

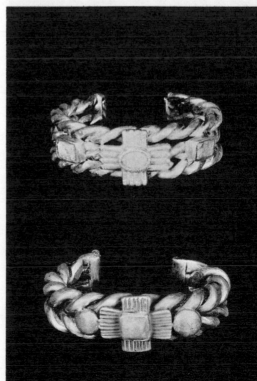

The wire comprised in these two bracelets was hammered into shape by hand. The uppermost is made up of three twisted pairs, the lower of but two. Applied by means of silver solder, various ornamental devices, both plain and set with turquoise, will be seen. Objects in which wire of this size was used are inclined to be too weighty for wear by the average individual. The lower of the two weighs approximately 5 ounces, avoirdupois.

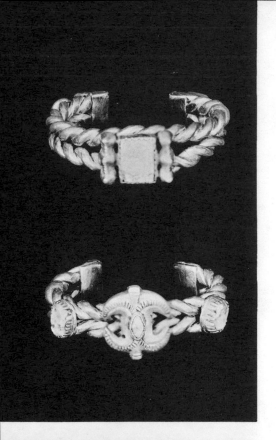

PLATE 3

Here are two more specimens of handmade, heavy wire construction.

The pair of nodular arrangements at either side of the square setting on the one above and the center ornament on the lower are of cast silver. These together with the several bezels in which turquoise has been mounted, were all affixed by soldering.

Besides the three sets visible on the one at the bottom, there are, in addition, others near either end.

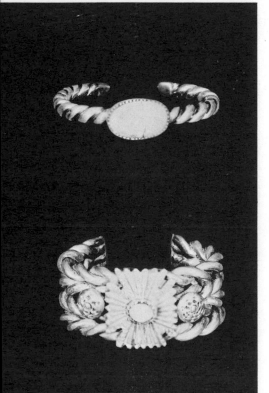

PLATE 4

The uppermost example figures an unusually conservative type of wire bracelet. A pleasing effect has been obtained by using a pair of drawn wires twined together, upon which an oval turquoise set has been seated.

Below it, a wider form is composed of three elements, each consisting of twisted pairs. In this, as in all others of this class, the cut ends of the wires are masked by plates of various sorts soldered to them. Again are to be seen the customary applique of independently fashioned decorative accessories.

38

PLATE 5

All the wire used in this pair has been drawn through a drawplate, a method taken over from the white man. The wider of the two consists of four members of two strands each, the narrower of only three, but of the same number of strands.

By this time, it must be apparent, and will become increasingly so, that those parts constructed of wire in practically all of the later bracelets, function chiefly as a somewhat ornamental base or support upon which a variety of decorative units can be applied.

PLATE 6

Several differences in the handling of wire work are shown here. Beginning with the topmost, four strands of twisted wire have been used in making up each of the three parts of which it is composed. In addition to the round setting of turquoise, two others, hardly visible in the picture, occupy positions at the ends.

The next in order shows the effect produced by twisting square wire, each of the three members consisting of but a single strand. The applied ornament with die impressions is mounted with a small set.

At the bottom is another triple arrangement consisting of a single round wire, on both sides of which are twined pairs of narrow flattened strips. Turquoise settings and cast, button-shaped objects, graduated in size, have been attached around a section of the circumference.

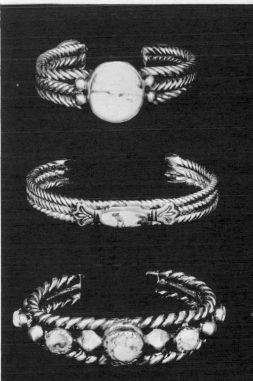

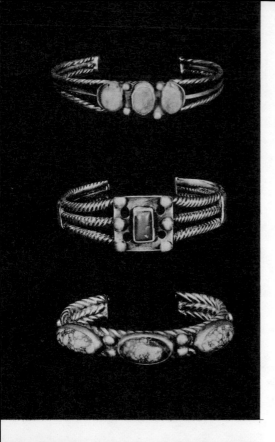

PLATE 7

Square wire alone was used in making up the topmost example, the two outer members being twisted, the central wire left unaltered.

In the one below it, an appearance of twisting has been accomplished by grooving the outer surfaces of ordinary round wire. There seems to be little reason for such an unusual procedure. The remaining bracelet follows the conventional pattern of two-strand twisting.

On all three of these are small globules of silver, formed by placing bits of metal in the desired positions, where they are fused, by means of a blowpipe, into the shapes seen.

PLATE 8

All of the wire going into these three pieces is of the square sort, twisted in single strands. At the top, besides the turquoise setting, four cast ornaments, triangular in shape, with nodular surfaces have been soldered on, two in front and two at the ends.

A narrow plate, supporting sets which are graduated as to size, covers the larger part of the w i r e foundation in the bracelet occupying the central position.

Below will be seen mountings of turquoise, fused droplets, and two small stamped devices applied to a tripartite foundation of square wires twisted.

40

PLATE 9

A curious arrangement of squared wire occupies the top position on this plate.

Beneath it is an example in which both top and bottom elements were made of round wire. Between the two is a reticulate pattern of very small twisted wires, only a portion of which can be seen in the illustration.

The remaining bracelet at the bottom possesses no unusual feature. The wire used was a twisted, single strand of the square kind.

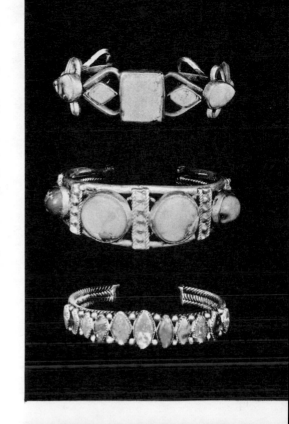

PLATE 10

Above, a light and graceful effect has been achieved by means of round wires in twisted pairs. Also included as part of the design is a contrasting figure made with a single strand of the same material. Toothed bezels hold turquoise sets.

Below, a combination of two different sizes of round wire have been used to produce a rarely seen openwork pattern. Note the extreme length of the teeth on the bezels which retain the turquoise in position.

41

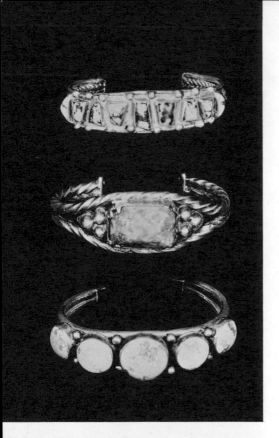

PLATE 11

Nothing basically different is figured here.

The uppermost example, constructed of both twisted pairs and single wires, is principally of interest because of the diverse shapes of its turquoise settings, all being of irregular angular forms.

Square twisted wire was employed for the one in the center. A large turquoise, cut by some native lapidary, and flanked by fused globules of silver, are prominent features.

Round wire was alone utilized for the bottommost example. Circular sets separated by pairs of globules provide the principal interest.

PLATE 12

Showing c o n t e m p o r a r y trends in style, the small bracelet at the top was made by flattening loosely twined sections of round wire, to which die impressions were later added.

The unique piece below it, contrary to appearances, is not a particularly late product. In this instance, a length of braided wire has been backed by a solid band. Nicely tooled oval bases support turquoise mountings.

At the bottom is another unusual form, one in which both single round wires and others twisted in pairs may be seen.

Zuni-style Bracelets

The above name was chosen for this class because the style is definitely known to have originated in the pueblo of Zuni, south of Gallup, New Mexico. It should not be thought, however, that every piece capable of being so classed was necessarily manufactured in that village, but rather that all examples, wherever made, tend to express something very much akin to certain decorative forms developed by the ancestors of the Zuni people. The predominant feature, one which is common to the entire group, is shown in a marked preference for multiple settings of turquoise, with silverwork usually of secondary concern.

This exuberant style seems to have come into full flower during the early part of the 1930's, there being no examples of record which can be safely dated much before that time. Curiously, nothing exactly comparable has yet taken place in any of the several developments incident to Navajo silver-craft, although members of that tribe accepted the new fashion to some extent and even went so far as to produce a limited amount. In bracelets of this type there is a considerable range in the matter of size and design, all the way from narrow bangles thickly studded with turquoise, to the larger forms, elaborately mounted with clusters of that gem.

Reverting again to the question of a probable source of inspiration for a decorative system which normally calls for such a profusion of turquoise, at the almost complete expense of the material upon which it is mounted, it can be pointed out that in prehistoric times, as well as in the first part of the historic period, forbears of the Zuni were accustomed to encrust various objects of shell, bone, and wood with designs in mosaic. These required, in the making, large numbers of small pieces of turquoise arranged in ornamental patterns. With this in mind, it seems not unreasonable to believe that similar effects in the silver jewelry of a later day would still have a special appeal to their descendants.

PHOTOGRAPHS BY STANLEY A. STUBBS

PLATE 1

The three bangles appearing here are typical of the narrower forms pertaining to this style.

A length of twisted square wire, often used by the Zuni smith to give an added touch, may be seen separating the upper and lower sections of the one at the bottom.

PLATE 2

For the upper example, three separate units were first made, after which strands of twisted square wire were introduced between them and soldered to narrow strips at the ends. Small silver globules were later fused in place in alternation with the turquoise sets.

Below is an unusually complex specimen of the same type. Note the small circular pieces of turquoise which have been set flush with the surfaces of the uppermost row of knobs.

44

PLATE 3

Three strands of t w i s t e d square wire form a foundation for the mounting of a series of lozenge-shaped sets, interspersed with small balls, in the narrow bracelet at the top.

The other and wider specimen, in the distribution of its settings, approaches a sub-style wherein the sets are concentrated into clusters. This variety will be brought to attention in a number of the following illustrations.

PLATE 4

Here are shown two bracelets on which settings of turquoise have been obviously arranged in clusters.

Round wire twisted in pairs, instead of the square sort, may be observed on the lower of these, while both exhibit much stamping as well as a variety of knobs and globules which were added for extra effect.

45

PLATE 5

Other examples in the "cluster" category are here illustrated. Silverwork is restricted in both of these to only enough plain round wire to support silver plates upon which bezels for turquoise have been affixed.

PLATE 6

The remarks accompanying the preceding illustrations will, as far as basic construction is concerned, apply equally to this plate.

A variation of procedure, however, occurs on the lower bracelet, where, instead of the more usual globules, four small disks have been affixed to the framework in a rectangular arrangement, situated close to the central floral motif.

46

PLATE 7

At the top is another design in the "cluster" class which has an effect almost like that of a piece of mosaic work.

Beneath is a bracelet form where a single twisted length of square wire once more is in evidence as a support.

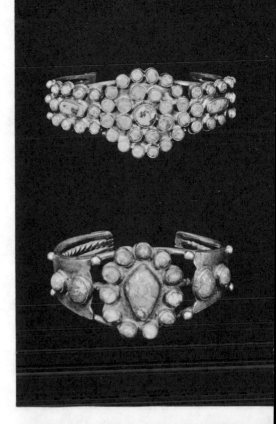

PLATE 8

A certain massiveness marks the two shown on this plate. A pair of small round w i r e s, twined together, have been utilized for outlining some of the larger features in the upper of the two.

Although the lower has a comparatively light and open effect, despite its size, it actually weighs all of 4½ ounces, avoirdupois.

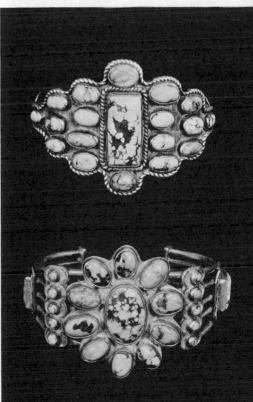

47

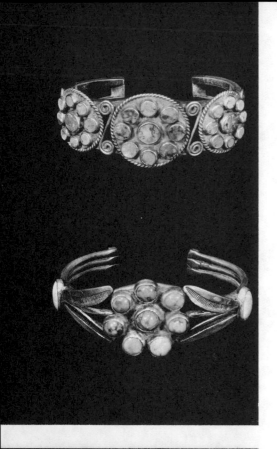

PLATE 9

Still coming within the group employing the "cluster" treatment, this pair calls attention to further variations in that general style.

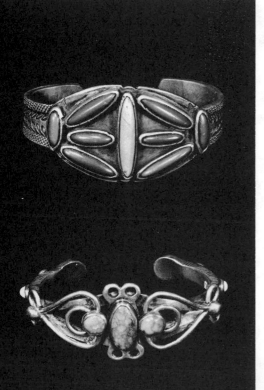

PLATE 10

While the upper of these two still adheres to the fashion for grouped settings, t h e r e has been, in addition, a great deal of tooling used toward the ends, which materially aids in enhancing the general appearance.

Seven turquoise were mounted on the lower one - those at the extremities, however, not being visible in t h e picture. Greater reliance was apparently placed on shape and a variety of applied devices, rather than a grouping of sets, to give the desired appearance of ornateness.

PLATE 11

When it became necessary to use fewer and larger sized stones to adorn their bracelets, the Zuni silverworker seemed to have felt that a profusion of detail in the metal work might compensate for a lack of the many small clustered mounts, usually appearing. This idea is well illustrated by a pair on this plate.

PLATE 12

Though less delicately treated in every way, the same concept, mentioned in connection with the preceding plate, will be seen to apply to both bracelets appearing here.

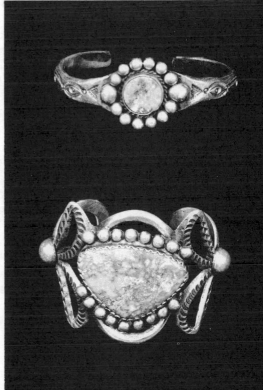

Wrought Silver Mountings for Wrist Guards

From time immemorial a necessary adjunct to any archer's equipment was some sort of a guard to protect the inner surface of the wrist from the recoil of the bow-string, following the discharge of an arrow. The Indians of the Southwest were in no way exceptions to the rule and for untold generations in the past undoubtedly wore on their wrists bands of leather cut from the toughest and thickest hides available.

With these peoples well-known penchant for ornamenting nearly every object capable of receiving decoration, it is more than likely that wrist-guards were not overlooked, though just what forms these may have taken has not been satisfactorily determined.

It was not until such protective devices, called *ketohs* by the Navajo, began to be embellished with silver that they attracted much attention. The fashion for metal mountings having once become established, increasing numbers of craftsmen as time went on seem to have vied with one another in giving rise to the wealth of decorative forms to be seen in some of the more inclusive collections of indigenous silverwork. As is the case with other articles of Indian metal-craft, brass and copper were sometimes resorted to, should the greatly preferred silver be scarce or unobtainable. While originally completely functional in character, after the passing of bow-and-arrow-days, wrist-guards continued to be worn purely for their ornamental value.

The accompanying illustrations show a few of the wrist-guards deposited in the Laboratory of Anthropology. These were chosen to give some understanding of the great diversity to be seen in wrought silver mountings. Other *ketohs*, bearing decorations cast in that same medium, will be dealt with in a separate section.

Photographs by Stanley A. Stubbs

PLATE 1

Obvious signs of long, hard wear, together with an elemental decorative technique, make it seem reasonable to assign the first example to a comparatively early period of silverwork in the Southwest. The re-used turquoise ear-bob in the center is held in place by a crudely made bezel, probably a late addition.

PLATE 2

Two separate dies and a cold chisel, the latter for making the lines dividing the field into horizontal bands, were the tools employed in decorating this *ketoh*. Information is at hand that would date the piece as a product of the early part of the 1880's.

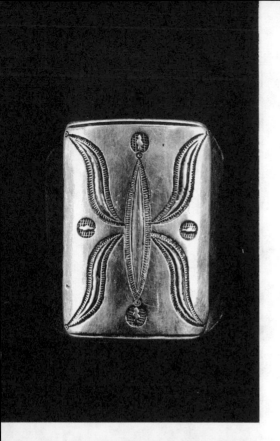

PLATE 3

Here will be seen, among other units of design, four of those bicurvate, leaf-shaped devices which appear so frequently in N a v a j o decorative schemes. Stamping, with a minor amount of other tooling, met all the needs in arriving at the desired effect.

PLATE 4

In this instance, an embossing of the leaf-shaped units and a scalloping of the ends create a novel appearance. In addition, it will be seen that quite a variety of dies had to be used to obtain the marked degree of complexity achieved.

PLATE 5

The central boss and four radiating elements, all in high relief are the most prominent features of this specimen. Around and between them are areas beautifully executed in a stamping technique. As an added decorative touch, the four silver buttons, seen in profile, were attached separately to the leather of the wristlet, to which the silver mountings was affixed.

PLATE 6

Another example of expertly executed die work is shown here. The leaf-like motifs have been embossed in low relief, while in the center there is a circular setting of turquoise.

PLATE 7

In this case, an unusually elaborate effect has been obtained by the use of numerous raised bosses of various shapes. There is also some stamping as well as seven turquoise sets, one in the center and three at either end.

PLATE 8

Fine workmanship and a nice appreciation for design are apparent here. As previously seen on Plate 5, a row of buttons has been added as a supplementary measure of decoration. A turquoise set also appears on this wristguard.

PLATE 9

An interesting variation in the structure of design appears-one where a central device in repousse and die work is surrounded by a comparatively wide frame comprised of impressions of several different stamps. An oblong turquoise set occupies a central position.

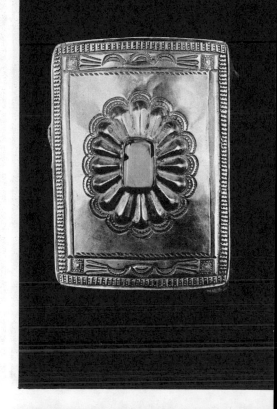

PLATE 10

The principal point of interest in this wrist guard is seen in the four groups of silver pellets which have been fused in place. The other features are not greatly different from some previously illustrated. An unusually large, almost hemispherical turquoise has been set in a toothed bezel.

55

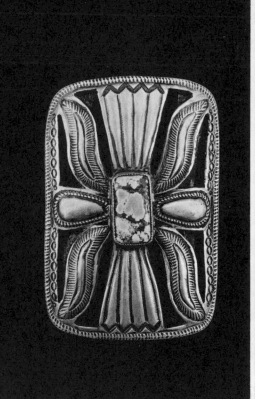

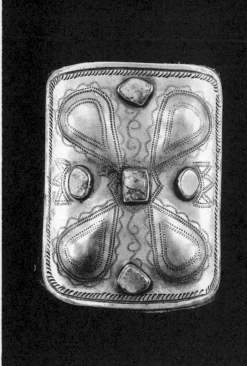

PLATE 11

Cutting out all but the decorated portions of an object was a rare procedure in Southwestern Indian silverwork. It is apparent, in this example, that the embossing and stamping of the design was first completed, after which those parts not so treated were removed. The usual turquoise set is present.

PLATE 12

Illustrated above is a *ketoh* exhibiting a most unusual treatment. Besides some embossing and stamping along the sides, all other decorative patterns have been made with some sort of graving tool. In this respect it appears to be unique. Five turquoise sets are also in evidence.

56

Cast Mountings for Wrist Guards

The remarks made in the preface to the preceding section on *ketohs*, as far as historical implications go, will apply equally here, but the type of work employed in their adornment is quite another matter. Although an elementary type of casting in silver was, without question, practiced by many of the earlier smiths, in that such a procedure was necessary to combine a number of coins into a single mass, ornamental casting could not have gained much headway until a sufficient time had elapsed to account for a period of experimentation. This being so, molded ornaments for decorating wrist guards must have first appeared at a somewhat later date than those which were wrought.

After mastering the technique of casting the more intricate designs in molds carved in stone, a great many artisans were in the long run able to turn out examples demonstrating highly creditable workmanship and extremely good taste. At times, for the sake of convenience, some of the more complexly designed pieces have been cast in sections, the several parts being afterward soldered together with such precision that close scrutiny is required to locate the joints.

Stamping and other tooling are not unusual accessory features used to enhance the general effect. Twelve examples, coming within this category, are figured in the following plates.

PHOTOGRAPHS BY STANLEY A. STUBBS

PLATE 1

The silversmith who designed this wrist guard took no chances with c u r v e s when carving his mold. Turquoise mounts have been utilized to break the severity of straight lines and angles, one in the center and four others at the ends of an equal number of short extensions. The connected series of embossed button-like ornaments at the sides are not part of the casting itself but are fastened to the leather wrist-band.

PLATE 2

A complete r e v e r s a l of thought from that demonstrated on the preceding plate is evident here. There is something not particularly Indian in the design, and it is quite possible that such a concept was the result of an alien influence in the past, as this is by no means a recent piece. The customary turquoise set is in evidence.

58

PLATE 3

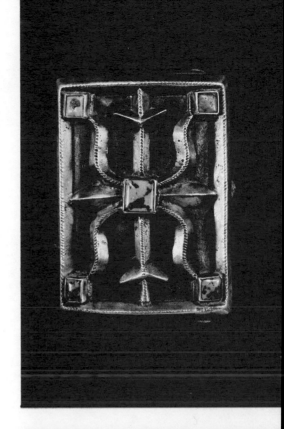

Extending toward the corners, from a square-cut turquoise in the center of a cruciform arrangement, are four curvilinear units. These were undoubtedly derived from those leaf-like forms which figure so prominently in a number of the examples illustrated in the preceding section. Additional turquoise settings occupy all four corners and a little tooling may be seen on some of the ridged portions.

PLATE 4

This *ketoh* seems to have been planned more as a means of displaying the possessor's wealth of turquoise rather than an attempt at artistic expression. Only enough stamping was applied to bring into prominence those parts regarded as forming a pattern of sorts.

PLATE 5

A peak in the art of casting in stone molds was reached when the example above was made. Objects calling for such delicacy of treatment were not often attempted if that technique was to be employed.

It must be evident by now that the four leaf-like units of design and a central turquoise set are so much a part of the decoration, normal to this class, that only deviations from the usual will be noted for the remainder of this section.

PLATE 6

One of the less elaborately designed wrist guards is figured here. Dignity and general good taste are evident, with no over-abundance of tooling to mar the effect.

PLATE 7

Cast in a single piece, the entire rim and the curvilinear elements were in this instance planned to appear in high relief, whereas those sections designed to receive die work are quite thin, more so than can usually be expected in a casting of this sort. An expert bit of work.

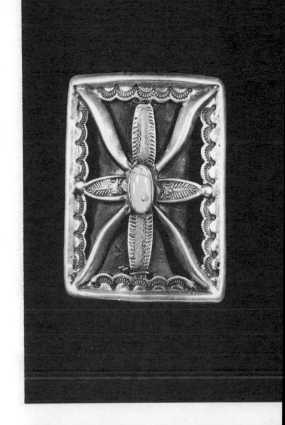

PLATE 8

The artisan responsible for this attempt must have been somewhat disappointed in the result. The lower right corner seems to represent the original intent but the other three show evidence of a breaking down of the mold, thus leaving no openings. No other serious flaws occur. Certain features of the design are atypical. To the right may be seen the edges of a row of 10-cent pieces affixed to the leather foundation.

61

PLATE 9

Aside from the fact that a particularly fine specimen of typical Navajo work appears on this plate. there is but one thing to note. This is seen in the hollowing out of the central parts of the leaf-like units. Considerable effort must have been expended in dressing down a rough concave surface as it came from the stone mold, especially when the limited means for doing so are considered.

PLATE 10

For this complexly designed *ketoh,* great care and a high degree of manual dexterity were prerequisites when cutting the friable stone in which it was to be molded. Any little slip while carving, especially one which would tend to weaken the slender partitions left standing for the separation of closeby sections, might cause them to break down under the heat of molten metal and thus spell complete failure.

PLATE 11

Two separate castings were needed for the completion of this example. The smaller of the two is comprised of the innermost oval, nearly obscured by a turquoise setting, together with its eight short, radiating members. The latter have been soldered at their distal ends to the inner aspect of a surrounding oval, thus filling a central opening left in the larger casting. So neatly has the soldering been done that only an inspection of the reverse side would show any trace of joint.

PLATE 12

Apparently some silversmith, in the past, became dissatisfied by restrictions imposed in designing the more conventional type wrist guard and then proceeded to experiment after the manner here illustrated. His efforts, however, do not seem to have met with any general approval since there is no evidence to believe that new trends in style resulted from his venture.

The *Najahe* Pendant

Far back in time and shrouded in the mists of antiquity a certain Asiatic people, authorities say, are known to have worshipped a nature goddess, one of whose attributes was a crescent. Somewhat later, probably originating from the same source, the Phoenicians of Tyre and Sidon venerated a goddess of fertility called Astarte, who was represented by a like symbol. As time passed the cult of this deity went with the Phoenician expansion, westward along the coast of northern Africa to Carthage and the surrounding regions, where their religious beliefs were no doubt imposed on the earlier inhabitants, among whom were the ancestors of the Berber tribes.

After the Carthaginian colonies were destroyed by the Romans (the worship of Astarte having probably also largely died out) only her symbol appears to have survived in the form of an amulet which was believed to carry auspicious implications. Finally the country was overrun by Mohammedan Arabs. But despite all these changes in religious thought, crescent-shaped charms have continued to be used to the present day by a population having a mixture of Berber and Arab blood, collectively known as Moors.

When, still later, a large part of the Spanish peninsula across the Mediterranean b e c a m e Moorish territory through force of arms, there can be little doubt that crescentic amulets accompanied the conquerors, some possibly as bridle ornaments.

Nearly eight centuries had passed before Spain was entirely freed from the Moors, in 1492. Meanwhile the local cultures became greatly influenced by the invaders. Among the styles adopted there appears to have been a type of horse trapping bearing a crescent-shaped ornament pendant from its brow-band.

It is not at all inconceivable that when Spanish horsemen arrived in the Americas they brought with them accoutrements retaining many of the characteristics derived from the earlier cultural blend. From such a source, without much question, the Navajo silversmith obtained the idea for his *najahe*, (nah-ZHAH-hay) that arched ornament which he uses, not only to ornament bridles, but as pendants for necklaces. Such, in bare outline, appears to be the history of what has sometimes been thought to be a Navajo invention.

PHOTOGRAPHS BY STANLEY A. STUBBS

PLATE 1

The fact that all of the older, simply designed *najahes*, of record, clearly demonstrate their use as bridle ornaments, seems to suggest a principal use in this capacity prior to their employment as necklace pendants. Two of this sort appear here. The lower of these can be dated early in the 1880's; the upper offers some evidence of perhaps being somewhat earlier.

PLATE 2

Both of the examples figured here were attached to necklaces. The pattern of cold chisel impressions on the upper one harks back to a time just previous to the use of dies for stamped decoration. The *najahe* beneath has been crudely set with pieces of abalone shell. As far as necklace pendants are concerned, the two may be considered as comparatively early forms.

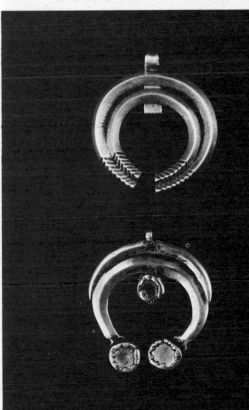

65

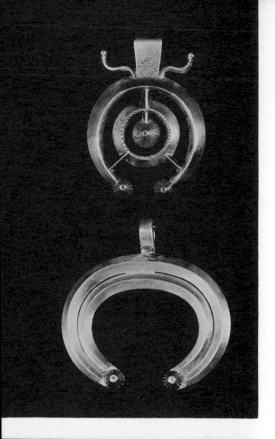

PLATE 3

At the top of the plate is seen an expert piece of cast work in pendant form. Some tooling was used to enhance the general effect. It was suspended from a string of beads. Below is an average *najahe* of the type to be found attached to bridles of more modern times. Note the comparative simplicity of treatment as compared with that accorded those intended for use with necklaces.

PLATE 4

The principal feature of the upper pendant consists of the two button-like objects with stamped design which have been soldered to the extremities of the *najahe*, thus virtually closing the usual gap between them. At the top is a twisted piece of heavy wire forming a loop for suspension.

The lower pendant, with the exception of the floral device at the top and a rectangular bezel for a turquoise set, was cast in a single piece. Provision was made, when carving the mold, for the series of small raised knobs on the disks at either end.

PLATE 5

In examining the upper specimen it must by now become apparent that in a majority of the later *najahe* pendants, most, if not all, of any original symbolism has been lost, provided that something of that sort was transmitted at the time of the adoption of the crescentic form. Four rectangular turquoise settings may be seen, two at the top and one each at the extremities.

Below is another variation. Again, the normally present central gap is closed, in this instance, by mountings for two circular turquoise sets.

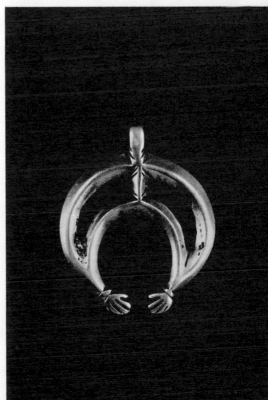

PLATE 6

Illustrated here is a cast pendant of the older sort, with ends terminating in miniature hands. There are certain reasons, at present not clearly defined, to think that these may represent a vestige of a symbolism which may also derive from an eastern source. A number of unfounded and fanciful tales have been perpetrated in the past by unscrupulous traders regarding the significance of this feature.

67

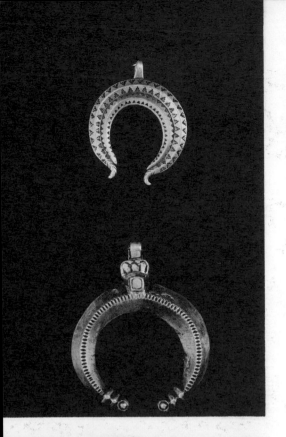

PLATE 7

The upper pendant is notable for nicety of workmanship and its out-turned ends. Below is an unusually heavy piece of casting with an odd treatment of the extremities.

PLATE 8

A high degree of elaboration distinguishes the two versions appearing here. A triangular turquoise may be seen mounted on the fringed ornament suspended below the center of the upper one, while three square sets of that same stone were used to decorate the lower.

PLATE 9

At the top is illustrated one of the newer cast pendants, the extremities of which end in variations of the hand-like concept noted for Plate 6. Although five digits are present, any actual resemblance to a hand is lacking but may hold significance similar to the one previously figured.

Below appears a unique flattened *najahe* form bearing a design in die work.

PLATE 10

Strictly speaking this pendant cannot be rightly called a *najahe*, because every trace of the crescent has been discarded But as a derivative form, it is included here to demonstrate to what extent any possible former symbolic significance has been forgotten.

Open-center Belt Conchas

Virtually every concha or disk of which the typical Navajo silver belt is made up conforms closely in certain respects to a single basic pattern. Both the oval and circular forms are alike in possessing a number of features common to all. These are: (1) a peripheral, sparsely decorated area with a scalloped rim which is bounded on its inner margin by (2) a narrow zone of tooling.

The various decorative elements on the outer of the two tend to be more widely spaced and more simple than those next in order, which normally are continuous in character, and occasionally are rendered in relief.

Such a uniformity of treatment argues strongly for an origin stemming from some particular ornament, or perhaps class of ornaments, seen and admired by one or more of the earlier silversmiths. From just what kind of object the style may have been derived has been a subject of considerable controversy, with much diversity of opinion.

A possible clue, however, has lately come to light in the shape of a pair of cast silver conchas of Spanish or Mexican workmanship (Plate 2). These were excavated in southern New Mexico, at a depth of more than 4 feet below the surface and were found in association with the remains of badly rusted spurs. In this pair may be seen the above mentioned outermost area with scalloped edges and an adjoining narrow zone of more minute decorative devices, a treatment which is, to all intents, duplicated on the later Indian belt concha. There is also a centrally located opening divided by a bar for attachment to a strap, which is again a prominent feature of the early concha of indigenous type.

Altogether, it now begins to seem probable that prior to the adoption of silversmithing by the Indians of the Southwest there had once existed in the Spanish colonies a fashion for ornaments embodying the three salient features just described. At this point, it should be remembered that anything resembling the open-work occurring in the unearthed example was quite obviously beyond the skill of any of the earlier aboriginal craftsmen. Hence, the later Indian borrower either might have taken over only the general idea, while ignoring that portion for which an ability to reproduce was lacking, or there could even have been a less ornate variety, within the same general class, capable of being more exactly copied.

PHOTOGRAPHS BY STANLEY A. STUBBS, UNLESS OTHERWISE INDICATED

A typical Navajo belt with open-center conchas.

PHOTOGRAPHS BY WYATT DAVIS

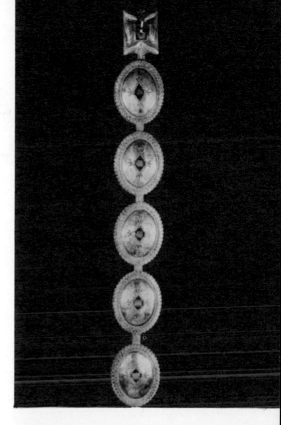

PLATE 2

Pictured is a cast silver concha of Spanish or Mexican deriviation, one which may well be a lone survivor of a once popular style. It is quite possible that from some similar object the much later Navajo belt concha was inspired. Although no small circular openings around the periphery are present, other features appear to have been preserved in the Indian type. Comparison with the following illustrations will demonstrate similarities.

71

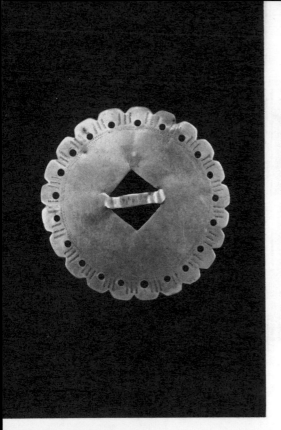

PLATE 3

By the late 1870's or early '80's the general features of the open-center concha had already become standardized. This is shown by a specimen of that period, for which an approximate dating is available. As in many early pieces, the impressed patterns used in decorating were produced by the edge of a file acting as a stamp. The thinness of the silver from which it was made also is an indication off the scarcity of that metal in earlier times.

PLATE 4

Here appear two of the later sort of circular open-center belt conchas. These were chosen for illustration through numerically outclassed by the oval forms, they are more nearly comparable with the one just described. Note that the bars dividing the central openings are more or less obscured by straps which remained in place during the process of photography. This comment applies to subsequent illustrations as well.

The principal differences between this example and the preceding is shown in a greater degree of elaboration in the treatment of the scalloped outer zone and the application of some stamping about the central opening.

72

PLATE 5

Oval open-center belt conchas exemplified here do not differ essentially from the circular sort in the basic layout of the areas intended to receive decoration. Such differences as do exist lie in the details of design and the character of the tooling. Some of these will be pointed out in the succeeding plates.

PLATE 6

Despite the superficial resemblance which is common to all open-center conchas, a close scrutiny will often disclose a number of well marked differences. In this case, note that the scallops tend to be more pointed than rounded, probably to accomodate the shape of the applied stamping. Also the design around the central aperture possesses an unusual delicacy.

73

PLATE 7

This example is distinguished by its proportionately small sized scallops, each bearing a tiny lunate impression. Slightly above and alternating with the latter are a series of circle-dot devices. In addition a stepped arrangement with four appendages surrounds the central opening.

PLATE 8

It would indeed be difficult to match the excellence of craftsmanship exhibited here. The die work is well-nigh perfect. Notice particularly the extremely small size of the perforations in the scalloped outermost zone of decoration. As usual, the open center has been outlined by a stamped design.

PLATE 9

Definitely departing from traditional procedure, there is a total absence of the series of small openings that normally pierce the inner aspects of the scalloped zone. The balance of the concha complies with standard usage.

PLATE 10

Heretofore, all the Indian open-centered conchas, previously discussed, have possessed central openings which were more or less of a diamond or lozenge shape. This may be considered the more usual form. But here there was an attempt to get away from the normal and to make it more of a decorative feature. To further this idea the opening has been outlined by incised, zig-zag lines, in order to secure greater prominence.

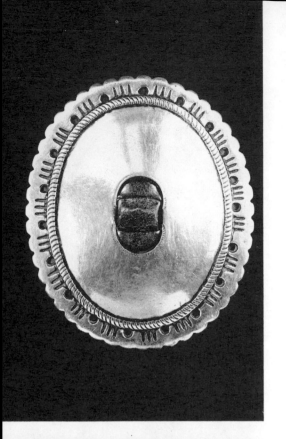

PLATE 11

Another aberrant form of central opening, one with rounded extremities, may be seen here. Openings having this form are rarely found.

PLATE 12

This is one of the open-center conchas of record in which areas other than those prescribed by custom have received tooled decoration. The four leaf-like forms are versions of those previously noted as a frequently used motif in the designs appearing on wristguards, both wrought and cast. See Sections 8 and 9.

Closed-center Belt Conchas

As time wore on a somewhat different style of belt concha began to appear, a style which was destined to supplant entirely the older open-center kind. The change appears to have come about because the cross-barred, usually lozenge-shaped, openings occuring in the centers of the old type concha greatly restricted the field for decoration.

Such a decided change can, without doubt, be laid to a progressive increase in skill and ingenuity on the part of the Indian silver-worker, who needed a larger space to accommodate his more and more elaborate decorative schemes. Notwithstanding all of this growing complexity of design the traditional scalloped marginal band and its bordering narrower companion were retained basically unaltered.

An interesting transference of function took place when the old diamond-shaped central opening, as a means of attachment to a belt-strap, was discarded in favor of a metal strip soldered to the under side of the concha for a like purpose.

Instead of completely abandoning the idea of a lozenge-shaped center, when no opening was longer a matter of necessity, the form was retained in the guise of a superficially placed decorative feature which served as a nucleus, about which a variety of design treatments were made to radiate. Less commonly seen are nuclear areas of elliptical or circular form.

In late years, because the typical silver belt was considered by many to be too cumberson and weighty, others with conchas were made, especially with an eye to the white man's tast. Additional late innovations include turquoise mountings and series of ornamental silver trinkets (see Section 16), designed to alternate with ordinary conchas. Only a few of the many types of design appearing on closed-center conchas can be figured in connection with this section.

PHOTOGRAPHS BY STANLEY A. STUBBS

PLATE 1

It is plainly apparent, in the concha figured here, that not only has the form of the erstwhile lozenge-shaped opening been preserved, but it has, with some elaboration, become the main decorative feature.

PLATE 2

The average concha is more or less dish-shaped, the belt attachment being soldered to its concave surface. This dishing is comparatively slight for the specimen on this plate. Several dies and a cold chisel were enough to produce the effective composition which surrounds the customary diamond-shaped center.

78

PLATE 3

A considerable amount of technical ability was required when this example was executed. After a preliminary shaping of the concha, the central part of the surface was filed away until the hexagonal figure, surrounding a lozenge, stood well above the general level. Radiating from the latter feature, beveled grooves were then filed, and finally a row of small triangular impressions were used to outline the entire central design.

PLATE 4

Here is a design which was based on a central arrangement quite similar to that pictured on the preceding plate. However, in this case it was not rendered in relief. The stamping has been accurately and neatly done.

PLATE 5

An unusual measure of elaboration distinguishes this piece, but despite the considerable degree of complexity, workmanship is excellent. Again a diamond-shaped unit, this time in outline only, is a central feature.

PLATE 6

Not only does a central lozenge appear here, but four others were employed in perfecting the decorative scheme. In addition, all five have been slightly embossed. A n o t h e r matter to be called to attention is the complete lack of circular perforations, u s u a l l y to be found in the scallop zone.

PLATE 7

Besides stamping and file-work, repousse was not uncommonly used in later times. An example illustrating the latter of these techniques is shown here. In this a fusiform element has replaced the more usual diamond shape. Another substitution is seen in the scalloped section where only imprints of a circular die mark the places where pierced openings more often occur. Two small holes, made after stamping had taken place, may be seen near the left margin of the concha. A reason for these is unknown.

PLATE 8

A simple but pleasing design is comprised of a fusiform figure which occupies the center of a slightly raised oval platform, produced by filing away the surface around it, and which constitutes the principal feature of one of the smaller conchas. Immediately above the peripheral zones of decoration, a beveling of the surface has also been effected.

PLATE 9

Another comparatively small concha of circular shape. The several members of the rosette, in die work, radiate from a rounded boss in the center. The lack of pierced holes in the scalloped zone must be viewed as an abnormality.

PLATE 10

A rosette in repousse, with no sign of any nuclear device. As in the specimen figured on Plate 7 of this section, a small circular stamp has been used to designate the locations where perforations customarily occur.

PLATE 11

The scallops on this concha were made to come to more of a point than usual, while again is seen an embossed arrangement for which no central feature was provided.

PLATE 12

In this instance all that portion of the concha bounded by the two outer decorative zones may be considered as a single oversize boss. In contrast, the peripheral portion has been very shallowly dished. A central disk in low relief, the result of filing away the surrounding surface, has been ornamented with lines made by a cold chisel which extend outward from the impress of a circular die.

Buckles of Wrought Silver

Antecedents of the average silver buckle of the Southwestern Indians are obviously European, so we can concentrate on the treatment chosen by the aboriginal craftsman. This ranges from mere copies in silver of the ordinary harness buckle to others where a large measure of ornamentation has been lavished. A few of the preferred styles of the past will be seen on the following plates, which picture only belt buckles, however. Small, much less ornate examples can occasionally be found attached to silver mounted bridles.

PHOTOGRAPHS BY RUTH BERNARD UNLESS OTHERWISE INDICATED

PLATE 1
Both of these buckles belong to concha belts of this early type. The lower, bearing a simple stamped design, is similar to the kind occasionally seen on bridles, although in such an event they would be somewhat smaller in size.

The upper is a copy in silver of an ordinary European harness buckle.

WYATT DAVIS PHOTO

PLATE 2
An oval buckle of conservative design appears at the top of this plate. Below it is another, the ends of which, at first glance, might be taken for repousse work. Instead, the rayed sections were actually produced by use of a file. A little stamping has been sparingly employed.

WYATT DAVIS PHOTO

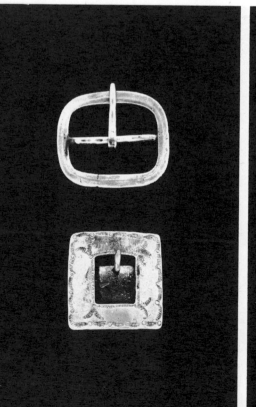

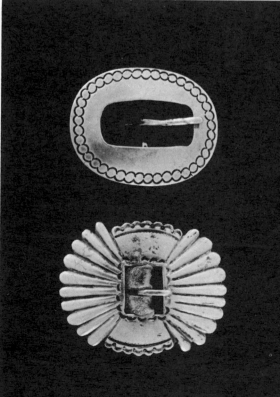

PLATE 3

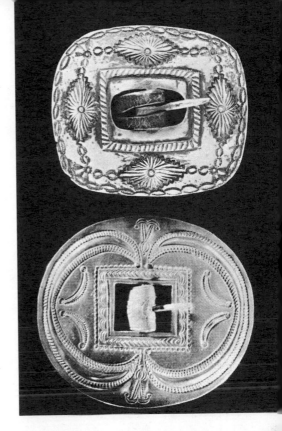

In decorating the upper example, the raised ridge of rectangular shape which surrounds the central opening was first filed and tooled into relief. Next the four lozenge-shaped elements were slightly embossed and, finally, dies of various sorts and a cold chisel were brought into action.

PHOTOGRAPHS BY WYATT DAVIS

The entire decorative scheme of the lower one was so planned that stamping was alone required. The maker appears to have been the possessor of quite an array of dies which he used in a very neat and efficient manner.

PLATE 4

Here, as seen on so many objects of Indian silverwork, are examples of that bicurvate, leaf-shaped unit of design which occupies such an important position in Navajo decoration. Two parts of these will be seen at top and bottom of this buckle. All have been executed in repousse. The stamping has no unusual features.

An unusual treatment for wrought buckles is shown in this illustration. All but the outer margins, two of which are wide and scalloped, is included in a single rectangular boss, rendered in high relief. Cold chisel and die work supply, in addition, a pleasing pattern.

85

PLATE 5

Upper: a combination of repousse and stamping in this fine example of Indian silversmithing demonstrates both skilled craftsmanship and dignified good taste.

In the lower piece an extra degree of prominence has been given the embossed leaf-shaped elements by outlining and covering their surfaces with a variety of stamped impressions. Two oval turquoise sets have been added near both top and bottom margins.

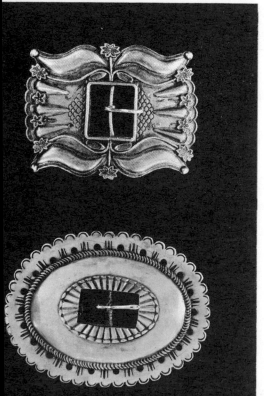

PLATE 6

Pictured above is a belt buckle, overly ornate by u s u a l standards, for which, in addition to the commonly used techniques of repousse and stamping, a form of overlay has been resorted to. All of the floral devices were made separately and afterward soldered in place.

On this last plate concerned with this section appears a belt concha converted for use as a buckle. Several of this kind are of record. The idea seems to have been to make a belt composed of an uninterrupted series of conchas.

Buckles Cast in Silver

Although the cast buckles conform in an overwhelming majority with the mechanical details of the European type, there are a few in this category that employ an entirely distinct method of operation. A reason for such a substitution seems to lie in the desire of some designers to dispense with the usual central opening, thus leaving a larger, unbroken surface for a further development of decoration. To accomplish this end, a procedure was devised by which one end of a leather belt is fastened to an attachment soldered on the under side, at one end of the buckle. At the opposite end, there is a hook-like arrangement which engages with one of the series of holes punched near the other extremity of the strap. An example of this variation may be seen on Plate 5.

PHOTOGRAPHS BY WYATT DAVIS UNLESS OTHERWISE CREDITED

PLATE 1	PLATE 2
A rather unusual form, as cast buckles go, is shown on this plate. Carving the mold for one of this kind should have presented few difficulties. A limited amount of stamping serves to bring into contrast the several parts composing the design.	The upper of the two pictured here is one of several made for a silver mounted bridle of braided buckskin. Beneath it is a small belt buckle of curious shape with a considerable amount of stamped decoration.

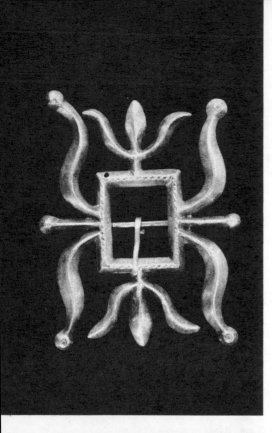

PLATE 3

This example, in general arrangement, may be taken as typical of many buckles of Navajo workmanship. The essentials of this particular sub-style consist of four of those ubiquitous, bicurvate, leaf-shaped elements extending out from an open center. In the spaces between them will be found a variety of design units. Plates 5-8 show other versions.

RUTH BERNARD PHOTO

PLATE 4

Although here the tripartite decorative compositions abutting on all sides of a central opening express the same general thought, the bases of two were made wider to accommodate turquoise sets, one a former ear bob.

PLATE 5

There is no central opening in this specimen, lower right, because it is one of those that operates with a hook on the reverse side instead of the more usual bar with a movable tongue. A large turquoise occupies the center.

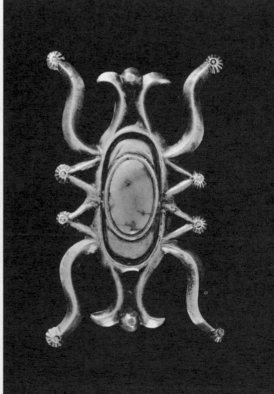

PLATE 6

The various members which make up this design project from a framed, widely expanded central opening, somewhat oval in shape. All bicurvate elements, instead of being attached only at their bases, as in most instances, are coalescent with the frame for about half their length, resulting in an interesting variation. Stamping and some file work add to the general effect.

PLATE 7

While conforming to a familiar pattern in a number of respects, this buckle possesses an unique feature in the treatment given the two cow's heads. These have been cast in *intaglio*, a technique not hitherto brought to attention in the literature on Indian silverwork. Evidences of tooling are very few.

PLATE 8

Below is an elongate version of a popular form of cast belt buckle. A good deal of emphasis has been laid on the applied ornamentation, executed by filing and stamping.

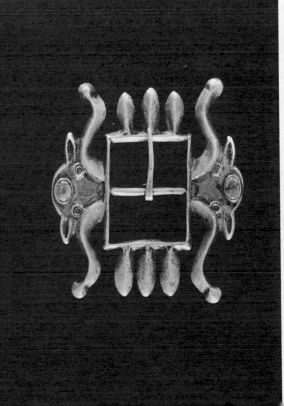

Buttons and Small *Conchas*

At the mention of the word button the average white man instinctively thinks of, first, a means for holding together certain parts of wearing apparel, and, second in importance, an article intended for decorative purposes. To the Indian of the Southwest, on the other hand, particularly those who still make some use of their traditional dress, just the reverse is apt to be true. In past Indian generations, such a view would have held even a greater emphasis, because in earlier times, the use of buttons as fasteners seems to have been almost negligible.

The first silver buttons, locally made, appear to have been shaped by forcing disks of that metal into hollowed out depressions by means of a die having a rounding head. This method resulted in a more or less dome-shaped affair. Later, the same technique was greatly improved and expanded by the native smith, who fashioned his own dies from scraps of iron, including such things as railroad spikes, old files, etc. With these simple tools, a wealth of pleasing forms were produced. In addition to mere shaping, as time went on, every decorative treatment known to the Indian craftsman has been employed to enhance the effect, such as filing, stamping, embossing and, in later years, even casting. A few of the earlier forms are shown near the top of Plate 1.

The principal difference between a button and a small concha is arbitrarily based on what kind of provision was made for attachment. Buttons are to be distinguished by a shank comprised of an eyelet or small loop soldered in the center of the under side, while conchas have, instead, narrow metal strips more suitable for the passage of a strap. Both terms have been in use for many years.

Due to a bewildering multiplicity of existing forms, as well as to avoid any charge of monotony, it has been deemed best to illustrate only a comprehensive sampling in connection with this section.

PHOTOGRAPHS BY RUTH BERNARD

PLATE 1

The dome-shaped buttons in both upper cornerss of this plate are of the earliest type and will again come to attention in Section 17. A flattened variety, notched around its periphery and next to that in the right hand corner, is also a very old form. Near the bottom is a small concha bearing a stellate design produced by stamping with the abrasive edge of a file, which well demonstrates an early method of decorating silver surfaces.

PLATE 2

All of the examples illustrated here have been set with turquoise. At the bottom center is an odd button which was tooled from a coin. The original imprint is still visible on its reverse.

PLATE 3

This illustration shows an assortment of cast buttons and similar objects. The centers of all have been mounted with turquoise.

Dress Ornaments and Allied Forms

The objects classified under the above heading, with exception of a single related group, represent an extension and a further development of the button as an item of adornment idea. Such a relationship is borne out, in a great majority of instances, by the means for attachment to fabrics which were employed. As in buttons this consists of a small loop or loops of copper wire. Occasionally, however, a crude pin-like arrangement of that same material was more rarely substituted.

This development followed no set pattern, but gave rise to a wide diversity of shapes and sizes. During the period of transition from the button stage, it was customary to make a number of duplicates of any given style, usually five or more, which together made up a set. The individual members of these sets were normally fastened at intervals along the lateral margins of those wrap-around, homespun garments which, in later years, were worn principally on ceremonial occasions. All examples on Plate 1, with the exception of the over-ornate specimen near the lower left hand corner, are members of such groups. Three others in this class are shown on Plate 2, together with other more elongate forms, designed to be worn either singly or in pairs. Incidentally there is an unrelated form of costume decoration consisting of a strap bearing a series of buttons and ending in some kind of small pendant. This sort is rarely to be seen in these times.

Although distinct in function, there is a phase which may well claim a place in the discussions pertaining to this section. Reference is made to those ornamental trinkets which are used in connection with some concha belts, in order to make for a more elaborate effect. They are used in alternation with the regulation concha. Because of a marked resemblance in general form and treatment with certain dress ornaments, it appears logical to believe that these additions to belt decoration were derived from some form of dress ornament. Plates 5 and 6 are devoted to examples of this latest phase. A comparison of these with some of the forms figured on the four preceding plates will serve to illustrate the point.

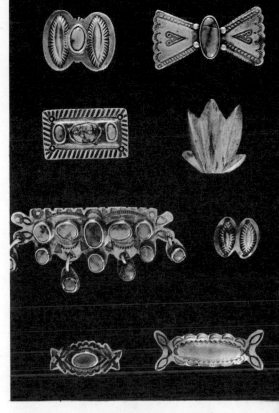

PLATE 1

As previously noted in the text heading this section, all but the ornament with the small pendants, appearing here, are members of sets, each group consisting of several duplicates. Such sets usually number up to five or more. Stamping, embossing, and the use of turquoise sets are all in evidence.

PHOTOGRAPHS BY WYATT DAVIS

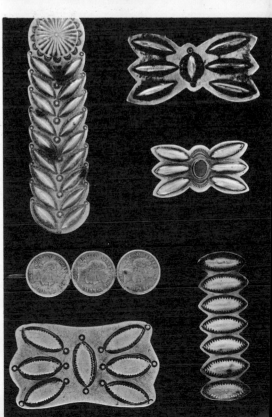

PLATE 2

In the upper left hand corner is shown one unit of a pair, while diagonally opposite is a smaller style, apparently intended to be worn singly. Also used for personal adornment are three dimes soldered to a length of copper wire. The three remaining items belong to as many different sets. Compare these latter with the belt ornaments on Plate 5 and observe the general similarity of form.

93

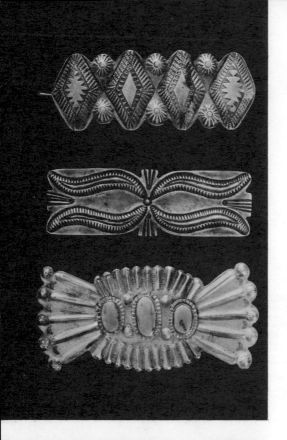

PLATE 3

Of the three figured on this plate, the two upper are typical of this class of object; the lower, mounted with three turquoise, on the contrary, is more characteristic of the over-ornate styles of a later date.

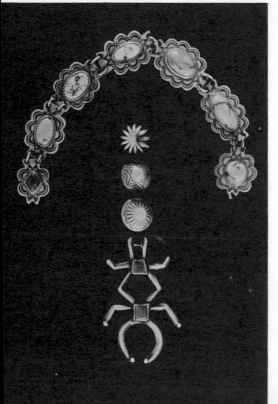

PLATE 4

At the top is another late idea for the adornment of clothing. A hook-like device at either end makes this linked series of units easily adjustable to any position. In this case the turquoise has become of greater importance than the silverwork—a modern trend.

Below, is one of those old-fashioned strap ornaments with a cast pendant.

PHOTOGRAPHS BY WYATT DAVIS

PLATE 5

Belt ornaments, or slides, as they are often called, may be distinguished from those designed for use on garments by the copper strip soldered on the rear for attachment to a belt. They also tend to average somewhat larger in size. Repousse has been extensively employed in the group illustrated here. A turquoise set appears in the center of the uppermost figure.

PHOTOGRAPHS BY WYATT DAVIS

PLATE 6

Here are depicted further examples in the belt slide category. Though some embossing is in evidence, stamping has become a more prominent feature. The example in the middle has been mounted with a turquoise.

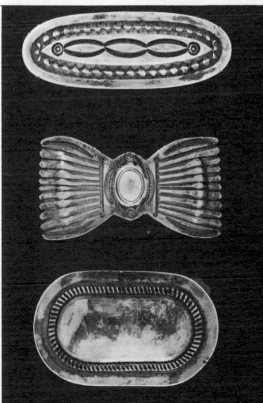

95

The Silver Necklace

Although nothing definite is known concerning the antecedents of the silver bead necklace, a few tentative clues have come to light. One of the most suggestive of these is furnished by an old photograph, believed to have been taken in the 1860's. This show a Navajo woman wearing a necklace of what appears to be dome-shaped buttons (see Plate 1, Section 15), so strung that alternate buttons face in opposite directions.

From this, it appears that these buttons must have been fitted with some sort of eyelet fastened underneath in order that they could have been worn as shown. This would in turn argue for a knowledge of soldering. Any progressive advance in the application of such a process would eventually make it possible to solder together the margins of two buttons and thus give rise to a spherical bead.

Today, as in the past, all beads are made in this same way, be they plain or ribbed. The two halves having been first shaped by appropriate dies, holes are punched from within outward for the passage of a cord and finally the sections are soldered together along the edges, the joint being dressed to smoothness.

Although ordinarily more or less spherical, beads show considerable variation, ranging from greatly depressed forms to those decidedly elongate in shape. Some of these are illustrated in the plates immediately following.

Because the Indian silver necklace is often a composite of several features, it has been thought best to treat in subsections under the general heading the components (other than simple beads) which may be found in certain examples.

PHOTOGRAPHS BY WYATT DAVIS

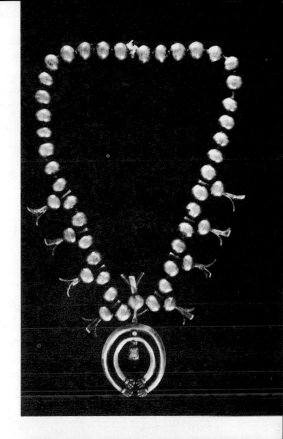

PLATE 1

A typical silver necklace of the "squash-blossom" variety.

PLATE 2

A few of the less common bead shapes are illustrated here and on the next plate.

97

Modified Beads and Other Decorations

The objects to be considered in this subdivision are those decorative items which are used in alternation with ordinary beads to enhance the overall appearance of a necklace. Of these, the most frequently seen are those beads to which have been affixed conventionalized floral representations or "squash-blossoms", as they are commonly known (see the accompanying plate). By whom and under what circumstances the latter name was first applied to these convenizations is a matter of conjecture, as the term has now been in common usage for many years. However, it is not believed to have been of Indian origin, nor is it thought that these flower-like objects were intended to symbolize the blossoms of the squash. As a matter of fact, competent authorities agree that the idea was taken over from a class of popular, Spanish-Mexican garment ornments which were stylized versions of the pomegranate, either of the flower or perhaps the immature fruit. Whatever the actual origin may have been, a wide variety of forms were, in time, evolved.

Also included in the modified bead classification are a few examples which deviate from the more conventional type. One of these, a variation from the pueblo of Zuni. displays a fleur-de-lis (Plate 3).

Among other decorative devices designed for alternation with necklace beads are: small Latin crosses, both wrought and cast; flattened floral motifs; miniature *najahes;* and coins of various sorts. The crosses were made by or for the pueblo groups who had, at least nominally, embraced Christianity.

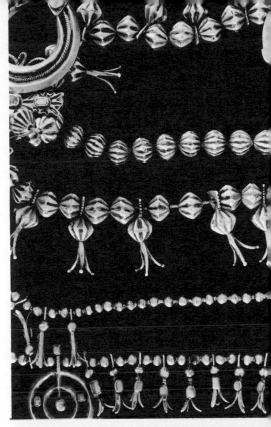

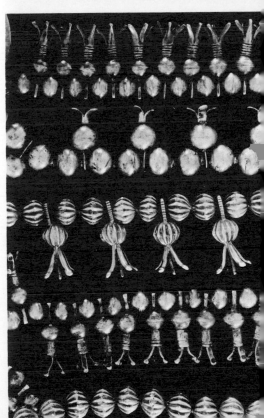

Here may be seen a number of beads combined with variations of the so-called "squash blossom" concept.

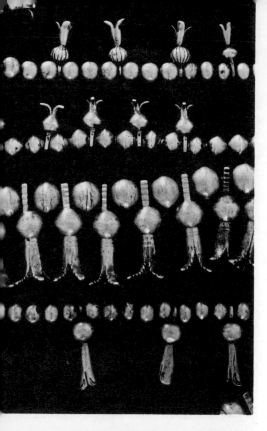

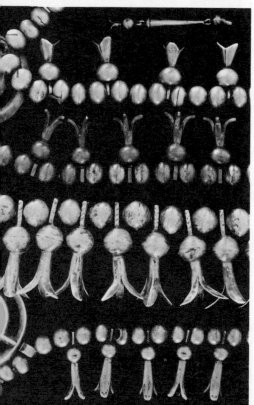

PLATES 3 & 4

The groups shown here are comprised of additional examples belonging in the same class as those figured on the previous two plates.

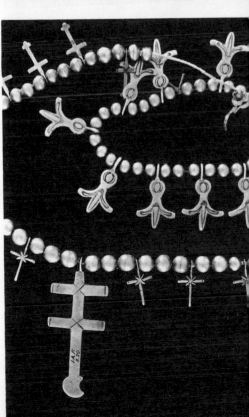

PLATES 5 & 6

Besides the more common modified bead forms, other kinds of ornamental necklace accessories are pictured here. Small Latin crosses were particularly esteemed by Pueblo Indians.

Necklace Pendants Other Than *Najahes*

Necklace pendants are so predominantly of the *najahe* style that the other kinds, as far as numerical standing goes, sink into comparative insignificance. Likewise, in this minority group the double-barred cross greatly outnumbers all others, so much so that at the time of this writing only a single specimen of anything out of the ordinary was found available for illustrative purposes. This one may be seen on Plate 1.

With regard to the double-barred cross, its use appears to be almost exclusively confined to the Pueblo Indians, and, among that group, largely to the more western villagers. This particular type of cross is usually thought of in relation to the eastern orthodox churches, but like forms are also known under the names of Lorraine and Caravaca, respectively. Many are apt to be puzzled by its appearance in the Southwest, as the form seems not to have had any connection with the religious orders dealing with the aboriginal inhabitants of that area. Nevertheless, two possibilities exist to account for its introduction.

The least likely will be taken up first. It is well known that the French of earlier times, in the more eastern and northern sections of the country, distributed Lorraine crosses to some of the Indians of those parts. This is proved by the occurrence of these crosses in native burials, but the great distance lying between that region and the Southwest with a consequent lack of opportunity for trade tend to discount the probability of its having arrived from that direction.

Another and more promising solution would involve an importation from Spain of the Caravaca cross, not by any religious order but by individuals. The characteristic form of this variety differs from that of Lorraine in having all of its evtremities end in some sort of ornamental arrangement. The example in the upper right-hand corner of Plate 2 fulfills these requirements. A reason for the occurrence of a double-barred cross in a country where the use of the simple Latin type is paramount is told in a Spanish legend.

In this tale, it appears that during the occupation of Spain by the Moors, a Catholic priest was asked by one of the high ranging conquerors to say Mass, but to the former's embarrassment, no cross could be located. In response to prayer, however, a double-barred cross was miraculously transported by two angels from one of the Eastern Orthodox churches to Caravaca, where the event took place, thus relieving an awkward situation. Here it has been retained ever since.

The preceding event, briefly told, is said to have taken place about A. D. 1232. For the several hundred years since that time thousands of replicas of this venerated relic have been sought out by pilgrims and travelers to ward off evils of various sorts.

When Spain began its colonization of the New World, there can be but few doubts that many of those taking part in the movement were owners of the Caravaca cross, which in this manner eventually reached Pueblo Indian territory.

Whatever the origin, the reason that this emblem was so readily accepted is very understandable, when it can be pointed out that an ancient symbol, having that same general shape, is involved in certain aspects of Pueblo mythology. To them the symbol represents the dragon fly, one of several animate forms having to do with water, always a primary concern with these agriculturists. It is therefore not surprising to find numbers of these villages, as in Zuni and Acoma, who do not hesitate to call it by its traditional name, though in other instances it may also hold some Christian implications . These pendants at times bear somewhat heart-shaped or crescentlike appendages at their bases, but what is intended to be represented (perhaps an exaggeration of some anatomical detail, such as an ovapositor) has not been discovered.

WYATT DAVIS PHOTO

PLATE 1 (Upper)
This pendant, as it shows no affiliations with any of the more usual styles, must be credited to some silversmith's personal fancy. An oblong turquoise has been set just below the point of suspension.

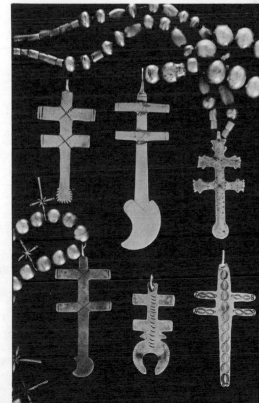

PLATE 2 (Lower)
Several versions of the double-barred cross are illustrated here. All but the example in the center of the bottom row are typical of this class. Notice the curious treatment given the lower ends of this and those above and to its left.

Finger Rings

The custom of wearing metal finger rings by the Indians of the Southwest, to judge from the earliest known examples, may well have been in imitation of European usage. A few plain bands are of record, as well as others with simple tooled lines or elementary stamped designs, all indicative of an early period. Very thin gauge silver was the rule during those years. A little later some were made to get the effect of rings bearing sets, with nothing but silver to work with; many proved quite successful Occasionally some of the baser metals, such as brass and copper, were also employed for this purpose. Still rarer are those comparatively early examples which were actually mounted with native garnets in the rough, bits of shell, glass, and other oddments, turquoise not being much used until considerably later.

As in other phases of silverwork, as time went on, a marked complexity in form and design progressively followed a like advance in technical procedure. An over-ornateness reigned at the expense of good taste. During this later period turquoise entirely displaced all other materials from which settings were made.

The last to be brought to attention are rings produced by the casting process. These are first cast flat, reheated and bent into a circle, and finally the ends are soldered together.

PHOTOGRAPHS BY WYATT DAVIS

PLATE 1

All the rings shown on this plate are illustrative of the older kinds. That in the upper right hand corner is set with the pointed terminal end of a rock crystal; the second from the left in the middle row, with glass; and the one below it carries a rough garnet.

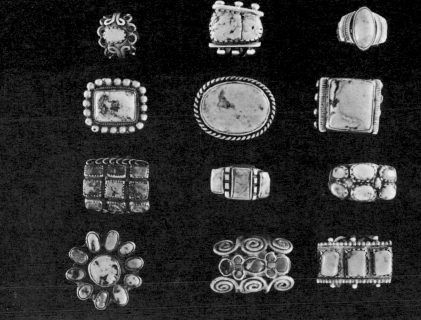

PLATE 2

A selection taken from some of the later styles are shown here. It will be seen that turquoise occupies an important place.

PLATE 3

As is demonstrated below, casting is capable of producing forms which are difficult or nearly impossible by other methods.

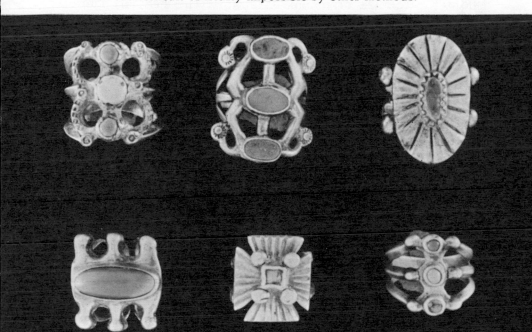

Earrings

With the advent of metal earrings in the Southwest, no new idea in the way of personal adornment was being introduced, but merely a change in the materials heretofore used for the same purposes. Although the general principle remained unaffected, a redesigning of ear ornaments became a necessity by reason of the nature of the new substance.

It seems peculiar that turquoise and colorful shell would, in the beginning, have become so largely discarded in favor of less showy silver ornaments, unless the appeal of novelty, or perhaps prestige value, as well as intrinsic worth, were being considered. Despite the altered standards in fashions, turquoise eardrops never became entirely obsolete, and are still worn to some extent to this day.

There now appears to be a backward drift in favor of the lighter turquoise ornament as against the heavier, more cumbersome silver article, except perhaps for that part of the aboriginal population which is subject to the influence of Zuni styles.

Another variety, having no connection with the earlier ring type, came into fashion at an undetermined period. It has a long, tapering, tubular shape terminating in a pendant squashblossom bead and constitutes distinct group. Just what prompted such a style is not known at present.

Although the Zuni people must have at first adopted and worn the simple hoop type of earring, the silversmiths of that community, as in many other branches of silver work, did not remain satisfied until they had developed a very distinctive and highly ornate class of ear decoration. A great variety of forms are included in this new division. There is also a lavish use of turquoise and a tendency to attach series of small pendants to lower extremities. These became quite popular, particularly among the Pueblo villagers in general.

PHOTOGRAPHS FOR PLATES 2, 3, AND 4 BY WYATT DAVIS

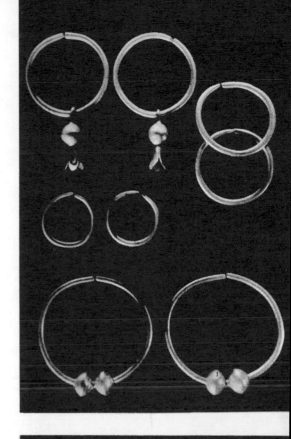

PLATE 1

This plate portrays specimens of the early heavy silver wire earring type and two of its varieties.

PHOTOGRAPH BY RUTH BERNARD

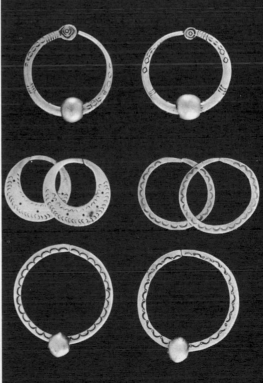

PLATE 2

At the top is a pair of earrings which, although presenting a flattened cross-section, have been slightly rounded. The remainder indicate no attempt to secure any convexity of their surfaces. An example at the left center is crescentic in shape. All have been decorated with die work.

WYATT DAVIS PHOTO

107

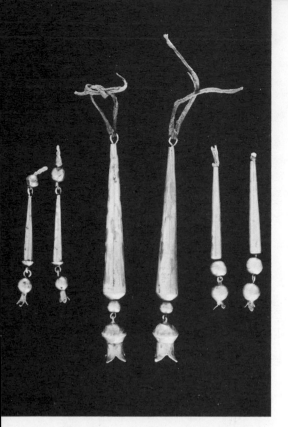

PLATE 3

A representative group of this curious form of ear ornament is shown here. The pair in the center measures about 4½ inches in length, and when worn would extend down on the chest to a point an inch or more below the collar bones. Narrow thongs of soft buckskin were passed through h o l e s pierced in the ears of the wearer as a means of attachment.

PLATE 4

Examples of Zuni style earrings are illustrated here. Notice the considerable use of wire and the small pendants attached to some of these - both characteristic of this type. In the lower left hand corner may be seen a pair of turquoise ear bobs drilled for suspension. but later mounted in silver to conform with a newer fashion.

Silver Mounted Pouches

To anyone who has had the opportunity of examining a sufficient number of old photographs dealing with Navajo life in the past a valid reason for the creation of the leather pouch, later to be embellished with silver, becomes clear. Even at as late a date as it first became possible to photograph members of that tribe, the scarcity of pockets in their clothes is most noticable. To what greater extent such a situation existed at an earlier period can well be imagined. Thus it seems probable that until white man's clothing became available, either for wear or for copying, pockets must have been few and far between. This made it almost a matter of necessity to provide some means for carrying about such things as fire-making materials, tobacco, probably a fetish, sacrificial corn pollen or meal, and other articles of daily use. In order to meet this, a pouch, with a strap to go over the shoulder, was apparently originated to fulfill such a need.

In earlier times it is probable that leather pouches received little or no decoration of any kind, but when Indian silvercraft came into its own, this was all changed. At just what time buttons, the first form of decoration, began to be used on pouches cannot be exactly determined, but it is noticeable that even the most simply adorned ones showing signs of long, hard wear were made from commercially tanned leather (Plate 1).

Possibly starting with a single button to hold in place the flap which covers the opening to a pouch, the idea of using larger numbers of these ornamentative devices grew, until not only the anterior aspect of the pouch but the carrying strap received equal attention in this regard. Although buttons were mainly employed, eventually both large and small conchas, as well as an occasional dress ornament (Section 16), were added to some of the decorative schemes.

In the older examples, the length of the flap was equal to, or even less, than the depth of the pouch, while those of a later date tended to have that feature greatly exaggerated in that dimension. Of course, the shorter the flap, the more accessible the contents of a pouch became; on the other hand, any lengthening of that feature would have an opposite effort. Besides these structural changes there was also a progressive increase in the quality and weight of the applied silverwork until, in the long run, the original function, as a substitute for a pocket, was largely curtailed. This was so marked that, in the end, the silver mounted pouch, with its shoulder strap, assumed more of the status of a conventional article of dress, not a great deal different from that of a necklace or other form of personal adornment. Such a change appears to reflect the increasing availability of a type of clothing with a plentiful supply of pockets.

PHOTOGRAPHS BY RUTH BERNARD

PLATE 1

All indications agree in pointing to a comparatively early date for the pouch shown to the left. An unusual situation is manifest in the total lack of any attempt to decorate the strap from which it is suspended. Length of pouch, $3\frac{5}{8}$ inches.

PLATE 2

At lower left is pictured a simple form with a rather meager display of silverwork. The buttons on the carrying strap are more widely spaced than was the usually accepted custom. Length of pouch, $5\frac{7}{8}$ inches.

PLATE 3

The large stellate button in the center of this specimen (below) must have been made especially for the purpose. Two nicely wrought, rayed buttons appear at both ends of the strap. Length of pouch 8 inches.

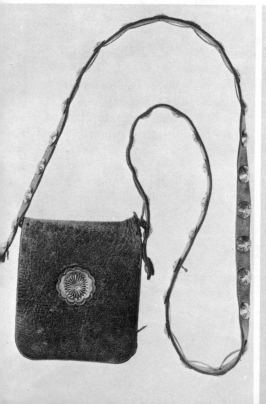

PLATE 4

Illustrated on this plate is an example on which, besides the unique central ornament, a varied assortment of buttons appear. The button attached to a buckskin thong controlled the distance to which the flap could be opened. Length of pouch, 5 inches.

PLATE 5

In this instance the flap extends slightly below the bottom of the pouch. Here the outstanding feature is a typical example of dress ornament which occupies the central position. Overall length 5¼ inches.

111

PLATE 6

Another specimen, with its flap some 2 inches longer than the depth of the pouch, illustrates the use of a large belt concha as the sole item of decoration. The concha bears an oval turquoise set. Overall length 6⅞ inches.

PLATE 7

The small concha, with the sunburst design, has a turquoise center. Altogether 291 quite quite small but perfectly formed buttons were used in decorating both the pouch and its strap. Overall length, 8 inches.

PLATE 8

This is one of those later pouches with an extra length of flap, more esteemed for its decorative value than for any practical use. Overall length, 8¾ inches.

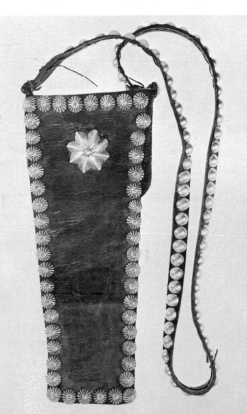

PLATE 9

A member of the long-flapped class is displayed here, in which the idea has been carried to the extreme. As may be seen, the pocket section, protruding slightly near the upper end, occupies only about a third of the total length. Overall length 14¼ inches.

Miscellaneous Silverwork

Included in this section are a variety of objects which were never produced in such quantity that they could be called commonplace. Some were in limited use at one time but had largely disappeared many years ago, while other forms, although later, did not succeed in achieving any particular degree of popularity. Today, items in both of these classes have become so rare that, in most instances, only a few examples have been found available for illustrative purposes.

TOBACCO FLASKS

The first to be called to attention are the tobacco flasks or canteens as they have also been called. For these receptacles there is no question of any but a direct derivation from a European source. It is well known that, prior to any attempt by the Indians to do silver work, similarly shaped tobacco containers were in use among the Spanish-Mexican population. These were fashioned from molded and hardened rawhide or, at times, from copper and brass. The Navajo smith merely copied an already existing form in silver but must be credited with adding decorative touches not found on the originals. Never numerous, these flasks at one time became practically obsolete, until, of late years, a few have been made, more as curios for the white man rather than for utilitarian purposes. An old flask and one of the later sort are illustrated on Plates 1 and 2 of this section.

GUNPOWDER CHARGER; TWEEZERS

The charger, left, is a relic of bygone days, when the only firearms obtainable by the Navajo were of the old-fashioned muzzle-loading type. These measuring devices were attached to the strap, from which the powder-horn was suspended, and held just the right amount of gunpowder required for a single discharge of the weapon. Although the idea of contriving some sort of measure for gunpowder would not

114

be unexpected, the Navajo form, with its arrangement for counter-balancing, may be credited to that people's ingenuity. These articles are very rarely seen today.

In discussing the tweezers, it must be remembered that many North American Indians keep their cheeks and chins smooth by plucking a scanty growth of hair which otherwise would appear as a very sparce, scraggly beard. Those who make their homes in the South-west are no exception to the rule. Tweezers of various sorts were used for this purpose, including such things as pairs of bivalve shells, possibly a pre-metal form. Brass was very frequently employed, but silver, by implication, may have sometimes been preferred as an in-dication of wealth or social status. The tweezers figured here were made from the latter material.

On Plate 3 are shown examples of each of the above implements.

Both of the objects appearing in the illustration have been decor-ated in a stamping technique.

MANTA PINS

Probably the least noticed articles of silver work, belonging to an earlier day, are to be seen in the manta pins, those adjuncts to old-fashioned Pueblo dress. This neglect is largely due to their scarcity, they being no longer needed when hand-woven garments were dis-carded in favor of more modern fabrics and fashions. Since that change took place, these pins have been gradually dropping from sight until but very few have succeeded in surviving. The manta, from which this type of pin gets its name, is a somewhat shawl-like garment, worn hanging down the back of the wearer, with the two upper corners brought forward over the shoulders and pinned to-gether below the chin. The four examples of manta pin appearing on Plate 4 have the pin portion made from copper wire filed to a point, though there are a few others of record having that part of wrought silver.

SILVER HATBANDS

The fashion for wearing silver hatbands is a comparatively late development which originated somewhere well up in the northwestern part of the Navajo reservation. Why the style was, at first, so largely confined to such a restricted area is a matter of conjecture. In this connection, however, it may be significant to mention that, some 20 or 30 years in the past, a trader or traders in that same part of the country had undertaken to dispose of an apparently good sized ship-ment of black felt hats, rather low in the crown but broad of brim. A good many of this sort were observed to be still in use in the mid-20's, quite a number of which were being adorned with silver bands. It might have been just possible, in the beginning, that one of the local smiths realized what a black background would do for this kind of decoration, but as it has not been feasible to verify such an hypothesis, no definite conclusion can be reached at so late a date.

A hatband consists of two parts, a narrow tooled strip of silver, sufficiently long to encircle the crown of a hat, and an ornament to hold the opposite ends of the strip together. Plate 5 figures a portion of two of these bands, at least enough to give some idea of their appearance.

AN ORNAMENTAL BACK COMB

At this writing the silver comb, illustrated on Plate 6, appears to be unique though unsubstantiated rumors hint at other examples, now lost to sight. It has been impossible, unfortunately, to obtain even an inkling of its past history. One thing seems clear, that is, its shape seems to suggest an inspiration from a Spanish-Mexican source. This in no way is meant to imply any considerable age. Since it shows signs of a fair amount of wear, including the loss of part of a tooth, it cannot be completely regarded as a mere curiosity made purely for a commercial purpose. In spite of some crudity in dealing with unfamiliar structural details, the workmanship shown in the decorative treatment is somewhat above the average.

MINIATURE SILVER BELLS

Among a variety of articles adopted from the white man and reproduced in silver, are those small bells, often referred to as mother-in-law bells. The later term is justified in part as it has been stated, by competent authorities, that, at times, some of these were worn by women to give notice to their sons-in-law that they were in the immediate vicinity. This was done because of the avoidance taboo observed by the Navajo. Bells of this same kind were also occasionally worn by dancers, and used, as well, for other purposes. An example may be seen on Plate 7 where a bell has been attached to a small buckskin bag which once contained sacrificial corn pollen. Besides the more conventional forms, there are others that are shaped like simple truncated cones. All types are furnished with the usual clapper. Very few of these are now in existence.

PHOTOGRAPHS BY WYATT DAVIS

PLATE 1

This flask was originally the property of an aged Navajo, once a scout and later a pensioner of the government until his death in the late '30's A chain, which keeps the stopper from becoming misplaced, is merely an old brass watch chain.

PLATE 2 (Below)

Here is displayed a comparatively recent "revival" piece. Expertly executed diework and a handwrought chain are plainly in evidence.

PLATE 3 (Below, right)

At the left, is pictured an old-fashioned gunpowder charger decorated with stamped designs.

To the right is an implement for plucking facial hair. Both this and the one, left, were designed to be suspended from handwrought chains.

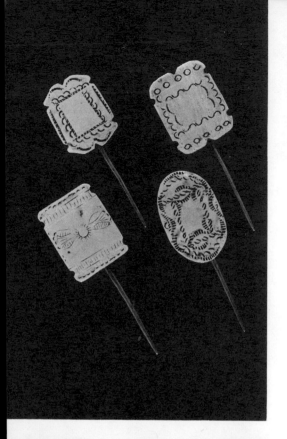

PLATE 4

A small group of manta pins are shown on this plate. Of these, three have rather crudely executed designs in a stamping technique. The fourth, at the lower left, bears, on the contrary, only a scratched decoration.

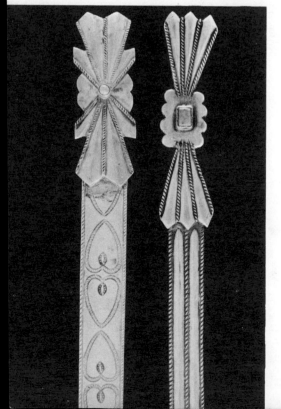

PLATE 5

Portions of two silver hatbands appear here. The one on the right has been tooled to give a fluted effect; that on the left bears a stamped pattern. It is interesting to note that the ornamental end pieces are very similar to some dress ornaments (Section 16), and both are alike in possessing turquoise sets.

118

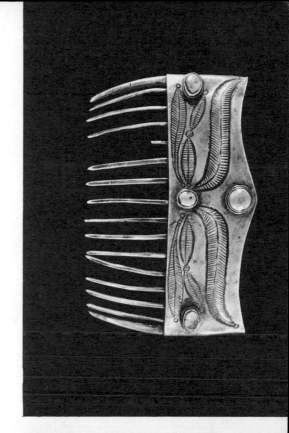

PLATE 6

This unique back comb, although of an alien form, has received a treatment of design that is purely Navajoan. The type of diework and a slight embossing of the leaf-like elements near the top are all characteristic. Four settings of turquoise may also be seen.

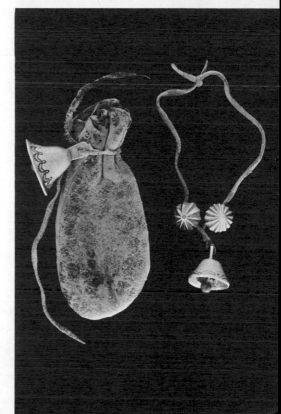

PLATE 7

Pictured here are two so-called mother-in-law bells, one attached to a buckskin bag, the other to a leather thong decorated with silver buttons. Both have been d e c o r a t e d with stamped designs.

119

Editorial Postscript

During the 20 years which have elapsed since the close of the periods so carefully described by the author there has been produced a wealth of interesting developments in Pueblo and Navajo jewelry.

To show these developments and trends, and to bring the study up to date along the lines of Dr. Mera's scholarly approach, will be the aim of Volume Two of this same title, which will be forthcoming shortly, it is hoped.

It is not true, dear newcomer to the Southwest, that all "Indian" jewelry is made in Brooklyn, Jugoslavia, or Japan. Only the junk comes from there - - there are now more good Indian artisans than there were 10 years ago at the time of Dr. Mera's Additional Note in his Foreword, and they are producing more and lovelier authentic items than ever before.

It is surprising to realize that the flood of cheap, machine-made "Indian silver" (despicable though it be) has not submerged the Indian artisan, but by furnishing to tourists an inexpensive introduction to a hitherto unknown subject, often awakens a burgeoning taste, and creates a broader market for good Indian work.

It is also apparent that the Southwestern Indian silversmiths and lapidaries possess an inexhaustible fund of versatile and ingenious artistry. They *can* grow in their own distinctive ways and develop from their own artistic bases without aping Caucasian designs. They have established and are consolidating a regional but internationally-important art, which will grow and change to meet altering conditions to remain a vital and permanent contribution to the richness of the world's diverse cultures.

Dr. Mera, bless him, would have been pleased.

D. S. K.

120

Index

121

Index (cont.)